Ultimate Reptile Care Guide

Responsible Ownership, Expert Enclosures, and Species-Specific Well-being

Ultimate Reptile Care Guide: Responsible Ownership, Expert Enclosures, and Species-Specific Well-being

Copyright © 2024 by Gerald Beathard III

All rights reserved.

Permission to reproduce or transmit in any form or by any means, electronic or mechanical, including photocopying, photographic and recording audio or video, or by any information storage and retrieval system, must be obtained in writing from the author.

Ultimate Reptile Care Guide: Responsible Ownership, Expert Enclosures, and Species-Specific Well-being is a registered trademark of Gerald Beathard III.

First printing February 2024

Library of Congress Cataloging-in-Publication Data

Beathard III, Gerald
Ultimate Reptile Care Guide: Responsible Ownership, Expert Enclosures, and Species-Specific Well-being / by name lowercase

Ebook ISBN: 9782544092420
Paperback ISBN: 9782136417150

Published by Royal Palms Publishing, LLC
Eva Myrick, MSCP, Publisher
royalpalmspublishing.com

Printed in the U.S.A.

Dedication Page

For my incomparable mom and beloved sister, whose unwavering support through the thickest of challenges has been my lighthouse in the fog. Your strength became my courage, your belief in me, the wings upon which I embarked on this journey of words. This book, a testament to the enduring power of love and support, is dedicated to you both. May these pages reflect the light you have instilled in my path.

Table of contents

Introduction i
Chapter 1: Choosing the Right Reptile 1
    Different Species and Their Characteristics 2
    Testudines - The Turtles and Tortoises: 7
    Crocodylia - The Crocodilians 10
    Gharials (Gavialidae) 12
    Considerations for Beginners vs Experienced Reptile Owners 12
    Legal and Ethical Aspects of Reptile Ownership 15
Chapter 2: Setting Up the Perfect Enclosure 20
    Types of Enclosures 20
    Size and Design Considerations for Reptile Enclosures 25
    Substrate Options and Their Roles in Reptile Enclosures 29
    Temperature and Humidity Control in Reptile Enclosures 32
Chapter 3: Reptile Nutrition and Diet 37
    Species-Specific Dietary Requirements 37
    Feeding Schedules 45
    Supplements and their Importance 48

Chapter 4: Handling and Taming Your Reptile................53
    Safe Handling Techniques 53
    Tips for Taming Shy or Aggressive Reptiles..................62
    Bonding with Your Pet..71

Chapter 5: Healthcare and Common Health Issues............84
    Regular Check-ups and Veterinary Care........................84
    Signs of a Healthy Reptile...96
    Common Health Issues and Their: Treatments 108

Chapter 6: Reproduction and Breeding 120
    Understanding Reproductive Behaviors 120
    Preparing for Breeding..128
    Care for Pregnant Reptiles and Their Offspring..........137

Chapter 7: Enrichment and Mental: Stimulation...............145
    Importance of Mental Stimulation for Reptiles 145
    DIY Enrichment Ideas...152
    Creating a Stimulating Environment 159

Chapter 8: Reptile Species Profiles 167
    In-depth Care Guides for Popular Reptile Species......167

Chapter 9: Legal and Ethical Considerations.....................192
    Laws and Regulations Related to Reptile Ownership 192
    Ethical Sourcing of Reptiles..193
    Conservation Efforts and Responsible Pet Ownership..195

Chapter 10: Troubleshooting Guide 198
    Common Problems and Solutions 198
    Troubleshooting Enclosure Issues 199
    Addressing Behavioral Concerns 201
    Conclusion 202

Introduction

Reptiles have long fascinated people around the world, offering a unique and captivating option for pet ownership. In this introduction, we'll explore the world of reptiles as pets, beginning with their taxonomic classification and understanding where they fit within the animal kingdom.

Reptiles belong to the group known as "Reptilia," a category that includes a diverse range of species, such as snakes, turtles, tortoises, lizards, and crocodilians. One defining characteristic of reptiles is their coldblooded nature, which means they rely on external sources to regulate their body temperature.

The history of keeping reptiles as pets is both rich and varied. In ancient times, certain reptiles like turtles and crocodiles held symbolic importance, often associated with power and longevity in various cultures.

Notably, ancient Egyptians revered crocodiles and kept them in captivity. However, the popularity of reptile pets truly blossomed during the Victorian era, when the fascination with exotic animals became a trend among the wealthy.

The 20th century marked a significant turning point for reptile keeping. Advances in husbandry practices and increased knowledge about their care made reptiles more accessible as pets for a broader range of households. This accessibility led to a growing appreciation of reptiles as unique and intriguing companions.

One of the key attractions of reptiles as pets is their distinct set of traits. They offer a low-maintenance pet ownership experience compared to many other animals. Reptiles don't require daily walks, grooming, or constant entertainment, making them an appealing choice for those with busy lifestyles.

Reptiles also exhibit captivating behaviors that can be both educational and mesmerizing to observe. Whether it's the graceful slithering of snakes or the deliberate movements of turtles, these behaviors provide insight into their fascinating world. Additionally, many reptile species have impressively long lifespans, with some tortoises living for several decades or even a century when provided with proper care.

One of the most exciting aspects of keeping reptiles is the diversity of species available. From the elegance of a ball python to the striking appearance of a bearded dragon, reptiles come in a wide array of species, each with its unique characteristics and requirements. This variety ensures that there's a reptile species to suit almost every taste and preference.

Responsible reptile ownership is a significant commitment that extends beyond the simple act of having a pet. It involves a set of ethical considerations, responsibilities, and potential effects on conservation and the environment.

Ethical considerations play a fundamental role in acquiring a reptile as a pet. Many reptiles in the pet trade are sourced from the wild, often illegally, leading to detrimental consequences for both wild populations and ecosystems. Responsible ownership means making conscientious choices, such as acquiring reptiles that have been bred in captivity or purchasing from reputable breeders who prioritize the well-being of the animals. This ethical stance helps in reducing the demand for wild-caught reptiles and discourages harmful practices.

Understanding the commitment and responsibilities associated with reptile ownership is crucial. Each reptile species has unique requirements for habitat, diet, and healthcare. Responsible owners invest time in educating themselves about the specific needs of their chosen reptile species. They provide suitable enclosures, regulate temperature and humidity levels, and ensure a balanced diet. Additionally, regular veterinary care and ongoing attention to the reptile's well-being are essential responsibilities that come with ownership.

The impact of responsible reptile ownership extends beyond the pet itself; it can have a positive influence on conservation efforts and the environment. Opting for captive-bred reptiles reduces the demand for wild-caught individuals, which, in turn, helps protect vulnerable species and maintain biodiversity. Some responsible reptile owners even participate in breeding programs aimed at conserving endangered reptile species, making a tangible contribution to conservation.

Furthermore, responsible reptile owners are mindful of their environmental footprint. They make conscious efforts to reduce waste and select sustainable materials for enclosures and accessories. Additionally, they understand the potential consequences of releasing nonnative reptile species into local ecosystems, which can disrupt indigenous wildlife and plant populations.

Reptile ownership offers valuable educational opportunities. Caring for these scaly companions can be an enriching experience for individuals of all ages, providing a chance to learn about biology, ecology, and conservation. As you read through the pages of this Ultimate Reptile Care Guide, we will delve deeper into the world of reptile care, exploring topics such as habitat setup, diet, health care, and specific guidance for different reptile species. Whether you're a seasoned reptile owner or considering one as your first pet, this guide aims to equip you with the knowledge and insights necessary to ensure the well-being of your reptilian companion. So, let's embark on this exciting journey together as we discover how to be responsible reptile owners and create expert enclosures for these incredible creatures.

Chapter 1

Choosing the Right Reptile

Selecting the right reptile to bring into your home is a critical decision that should align with your lifestyle, preferences, and capabilities. One of the first considerations is the size and space requirements of the reptile. Some reptiles, like tiny geckos or small snakes, require less room, while others, such as large pythons or iguanas, need spacious enclosures. It's essential to ensure that you can comfortably accommodate the reptile's size needs within your living space.

Another factor to weigh is the activity level of the reptile. Consider your desired level of interaction and engagement with your pet. Some reptiles, like turtles or tortoises, are more sedentary, spending much of their time basking or resting. In contrast, species like bearded dragons or corn snakes are more active and often enjoy interaction with their owners. Your personal preference for a more active or low-maintenance pet will influence your choice.

Handling preferences are another important consideration. Not all reptiles are equally tolerant of human interaction. Some species, like ball pythons or leopard geckos, are generally docile and handle well, making them suitable choices for beginners or those who enjoy regular interaction with their pets. However, other species may be more skittish or less amenable to handling, which should be taken into account based on your comfort level.

Different Species and Their Characteristics

Squamata - The Lizards and Snakes

The family Squamata is a diverse group of reptiles encompassing both lizards and snakes. Each species within this family exhibits unique characteristics, behaviors, and care requirements.

Lizards (Lacertilia)

Lizards are a remarkably diverse group in terms of size, behavior, and habitat. They range from tiny geckos that can fit in the palm of your hand to large, arboreal iguanas that inhabit tropical rainforests. Lizards have distinct features such as elongated bodies, typically four legs, and well-developed senses, particularly sight and smell. They vary in diet, with some species being herbivores, some insectivores and other omnivores.

Bearded Dragon (Pogona spp.)

Bearded dragons are known for their friendly disposition and enjoy human interaction. They grow to about 18-

22 inches in length and require a warm, spacious enclosure. Their diet includes a mixture of insects and vegetables.

Chameleon (Chamaeleonidae)

Chameleons are renowned for their color-changing abilities and unique eyes. Veiled Chameleons (Chamaeleo calyptratus) and Panther Chameleons (Furcifer pardalis) are popular in the pet trade. Chameleons thrive in tall, screened enclosures with abundant foliage, high humidity, and a diet consisting of insects.

Green Anole (Anolis carolinensis)

Green anoles, also known as Carolina anoles, are small, arboreal lizards native to the south-eastern United States. These captivating reptiles are beloved for their remarkable ability to change color, often displaying vibrant shades of green and brown to blend in with their surroundings. When it comes to their enclosure needs, green anoles thrive in a setup that resembles the habitat of chameleons. A tall, well-ventilated enclosure with plenty of vertical space is essential to accommodate their arboreal lifestyle.

Leopard Gecko (Eublepharis macularius)

Leopard geckos are small and gentle reptiles, making them an excellent choice for beginners. They typically measure 6-10 inches in length and thrive in dry, desert-like environments.

Blue-Tongued Skink (Tiliqua spp.)

Blue-tongued skinks are characterized by their striking blue tongues. They are medium-sized, growing up to 18-24 inches. These skinks need a spacious enclosure with a basking area, and they primarily feed on a varied diet that includes vegetables and protein.

Snakes (Serpentes)

Snakes are legless reptiles with a unique mode of locomotion characterized by undulating movements. They have evolved to inhabit various environments, from the underground burrows of blind snakes to the treetops where arboreal species like tree pythons reside. Snakes exhibit an impressive array of adaptations, including venomous fangs in some species, constriction abilities in others, and exceptional camouflage. Their diets are equally diverse, ranging from rodents and insects to other reptiles and amphibians.

Ball Python (Python regius)

Ball pythons are beloved for their docile nature and manageable size, typically reaching 3-4 feet in length. It's important to note that while males usually stay within the 3-4 feet range, females have the potential to grow slightly larger, with some reaching lengths of up to 5-6 feet (150-180 cm). They are ideal for beginners and thrive in warm, humid habitats.

Their diet mainly consists of rodents.

Reticulated Python (Python reticulatus)

Reticulated pythons are known for their impressive size and striking patterns. They are one of the largest snake species in the world, with adults typically reaching lengths between 10 to 20 feet (3 to 6 meters). Due to their substantial size, reticulated pythons require ample space and are not recommended for beginners. These pythons thrive in warm and humid environments, and providing them with a large, well-ventilated enclosure is essential for their well-being. Their diet mainly consists of appropriately sized mammals, such as rabbits or larger rodents, to meet their nutritional needs.

Burmese Python (Python bivittatus)

Burmese pythons are another popular python species in the pet trade. They are slightly smaller than reticulated pythons but can still reach impressive lengths of 12 to 18 feet (3.5 to 5.5 meters). While not as large as reticulated pythons, they still require a spacious enclosure as they grow. Burmese pythons are generally known for their docile nature, making them suitable for experienced reptile keepers. Similar to other python species, they thrive in warm, humid environments. Their diet primarily consists of appropriately sized mammals, and their enclosures should be equipped with proper heating and humidity control to ensure their well-being.

Corn Snake (Pantherophis guttatus)

Corn snakes, adorned with vibrant colors, are non-venomous and moderate in size, usually measuring 3-5 feet. They are skilled climbers and are often found in wooded regions, necessitating habitats with branches and hiding spots.

Boa Constrictor (Boa constrictor)

Boa constrictors are renowned for their imposing size, with some individuals exceeding 6-10 feet. To accommodate their large frames, they require spacious enclosures. Their diet consists mainly of appropriately sized prey like rodents.

King Cobra (Ophiophagus hannah)

The king cobra is the longest venomous snake in the world, capable of reaching lengths of over 18 feet. These snakes demand secure enclosures, and their venom makes them a challenging choice for experienced keepers only.

Western Diamondback Rattlesnake (Crotalus atrox)

This venomous rattlesnake is found in southwestern North America. It requires a secure and well-ventilated enclosure with a suitable temperature gradient. Due to its venomous nature, it is strictly for experienced keepers and institutions.

Testudines - The Turtles and Tortoises:

The family Testudines includes both turtles and tortoises, all of which share the distinctive feature of a bony, protective shell. Different species have adapted to various environments, each with its specific care needs.

Turtles (Chelonia)

Turtles are primarily adapted for life in water. They possess webbed feet or flippers for swimming and streamlined shells that aid in buoyancy. Sea turtles, in particular, undertake long migrations between their nesting and feeding grounds. Freshwater turtles are often found in ponds, lakes, and rivers. Turtles are known for their ability to retract their limbs and head into their shells for protection.

Red-Eared Slider (Trachemys scripta elegans)

Red-eared sliders are popular pet turtles known for their vibrant red markings. They require well-maintained aquatic habitats with basking areas. Their diet includes both aquatic plants and protein-based foods.

Painted Turtle (Chrysemys picta)

Painted turtles are native to North America and are known for their colorful markings. They thrive in freshwater environments and need access to basking areas and a varied diet consisting of aquatic plants and small prey.

Box Turtle (Terrapene spp.)

Box turtles are terrestrial turtles with a hinged plastron that allows them to close themselves off for protection. They are often kept as pets due to their manageable size and charming personalities. They require a varied diet and a suitable outdoor enclosure if possible.

Musk Turtle (Sternotherus spp.)

Musk turtles are small, aquatic turtles known for their musky odor. They require a well-maintained aquatic habitat with clean water and a diet that includes both aquatic plants and small prey.

Common Snapping Turtle (Chelydra serpentina) and Alligator Snapping Turtle (Macroclemys temminckii)

Common snapping turtles and alligator snapping turtles are remarkable aquatic reptiles found in various regions of North America. Common snapping turtles typically grow to sizes ranging from 8 to 18 inches, while alligator snapping turtles can reach lengths between 13 and 30 inches. These turtles are known for their impressive size, unique appearance, and fascinating behaviors in the wild.

Tortoises (Testudinidae)

Tortoises are terrestrial reptiles adapted for life on land. They have thick, dome-shaped shells and sturdy limbs, making them excellent walkers. Tortoises are typically herbivorous, grazing on vegetation in their arid habitats.

Aldabra Tortoise (Aldabrachelys gigantea)

Aldabra tortoises rank among the largest tortoise species in the world, with some individuals surpassing 4 feet. They require ample space and a diet of leafy greens and fruits.

Greek Tortoise (Testudo graeca)

Greek tortoises are smaller in size, typically measuring 5-8 inches in length. They thrive in arid environments and feed on greens and vegetables.

Russian Tortoise (Agrionemys horsfieldii)

Russian tortoises are terrestrial turtles, and they are relatively small, growing to 6-8 inches in length. They thrive in dry, arid environments and primarily feed on leafy greens.

Indian Star Tortoise (Geochelone elegans)

Indian star tortoises are known for their striking star-like patterns on their shells. They require a warm, arid environment and feed on a diet consisting of leafy greens and occasional fruits.

Marginated Tortoise (Testudo marginata)

Marginated tortoises are medium-sized tortoises known for the serrated edges on their shells. They thrive in Mediterranean climates and feed on a diet of greens and vegetables.

Spurred Tortoise (Sulcata tortoise)

Spurred tortoises, also known as African spurred tortoises, are among the largest species of land tortoises in the world, with some individuals reaching lengths of over 30 inches (75 cm) and weighing more than 100 pounds (45 kg). Native to the arid regions of northern Africa, they are well-adapted to survive in harsh desert environments.

In the wild, spurred tortoises graze on a diet of fibrous plants and vegetation, and they are excellent diggers, creating deep burrows to escape extreme temperatures. Captivity often fails to provide the expansive space and environmental conditions they require.

Additionally, these tortoises have the potential to outlive their owners, with lifespans of up to 70 years or more, making them a long-term commitment that not everyone can accommodate.

Crocodylia - The Crocodilians

Crocodylia is a family that comprises some of the largest and most formidable reptiles on Earth, including crocodiles, alligators, and caimans. These semi-aquatic reptiles are known for their powerful jaws, streamlined bodies, and remarkable adaptability to aquatic environments.

Crocodiles (Crocodylidae)

Crocodiles are large and heavily armored reptiles that inhabit a variety of freshwater and brackish habitats, from rivers and swamps to estuaries. They are formidable predators with V-shaped snouts and a diverse diet that may include fish, mammals, and birds. Crocodiles are known for their patient and stealthy hunting strategies.

Nile Crocodile (Crocodylus niloticus)

Nile crocodiles are known for their aggression and formidable size, growing up to 16-20 feet in length. They thrive in expansive aquatic habitats and predominantly consume fish and meat.

Saltwater Crocodile (Crocodylus porosus)

Saltwater crocodiles are renowned for their territorial behavior and adaptability to saltwater environments. They are the largest living reptiles and are known for their impressive size and strength.

Alligators and Caimans (Alligatoridae)

Alligators and caimans are closely related to crocodiles and share many similarities. They are characterized by Ushaped snouts and are often found in freshwater habitats, including swamps and marshes. While they share some habits with crocodiles, they are generally considered less aggressive.

American Alligator (Alligator mississippiensis)

American alligators are found in the southeastern United States and can reach lengths of 13-15 feet. They require spacious enclosures with access to water and primarily feed on fish and meat.

Spectacled Caiman (Caiman crocodilus)

Spectacled caimans are smaller in size and inhabit a variety of freshwater environments in Central and South America. They have distinctive bony plates on their skin and a diet that includes fish and small mammals.

Gharials (Gavialidae)

Gharials are unique crocodilians characterized by their long, slender snouts filled with sharp teeth. They are specialized fish-eaters and are found in the rivers of India and Nepal. Gharials are critically endangered, with only a few remaining populations.

Indian Gharial (Gavialis gangeticus)

Indian gharials are known for their distinctive appearance, with elongated snouts studded with numerous sharp teeth. They are primarily fish-eaters and are adapted to life in fast-flowing rivers. Due to their endangered status, they are subject to strict conservation efforts and are not typically kept as pets.

Each reptile family offers a wide range of species, each with its unique behavioral traits, size variations, and specific care needs. Understanding the specific requirements of these species is essential for providing them with the best possible care and ensuring their well-being in captivity. Whether you're a beginner or an experienced reptile keeper, there's a fascinating array of reptiles to explore and appreciate within the Squamata and

Testudines families.

Considerations for Beginners vs Experienced Reptile Owners

Reptile ownership encompasses a fascinating spectrum of experiences, catering to individuals with varying levels of expertise. It is a journey filled with unique challenges and rewards, and the considerations surrounding reptile ownership differ significantly between beginners and experienced reptile owners. Whether one is embarking on their initial foray into reptile-keeping or possesses a wealth of knowledge gained through years of experience, comprehending the distinct facets of reptile ownership tailored to their expertise level is paramount.

For beginners, the process often commences with selecting an appropriate starter species, a critical first step in this fascinating journey. The choice of a beginner friendly reptile species sets the foundation for a successful and enjoyable experience. Various factors must be considered during this selection process.

These include the size of the reptile, its temperament, dietary preferences, specific enclosure requirements, healthcare needs, expected lifespan, and compliance with local legal regulations. It is advisable for beginners to commence their journey with species known for their ease of care, tolerance for minor errors,

and straightforward care demands. As beginners gain experience and confidence, they can progressively explore more challenging species with specific care prerequisites.

In contrast, experienced reptile owners venture into the realm of reptile ownership with a different set of considerations. They are often drawn to the unique challenges and rewards that come with their advanced expertise. These challenges may encompass the care of species with specialized requirements, such as chameleons or venomous snakes. Successful management of these reptiles necessitates an in-depth understanding of their distinct habitat preferences, dietary habits, and behavioral patterns.

Additionally, experienced reptile keepers may delve into reptile breeding programs, a complex undertaking that encompasses creating optimal breeding conditions and providing meticulous care to hatchlings. Some also engage in conservation efforts, collaborating with endangered species or participating in breeding initiatives that contribute to broader conservation goals.

The rewards of reptile ownership for experienced keepers are equally profound. They often invest in intricate and custom designed enclosures, integrating natural elements to craft enriched environments for their reptiles. Furthermore, their extensive knowledge allows them to educate others about reptiles and advocate for their welfare, making significant contributions to the broader reptile-keeping community. The sense of achievement derived from successfully caring for and breeding reptiles, particularly those with intricate care requirements, further enhances the fulfilment experienced reptile owners derive from their chosen passion.

Irrespective of their level of experience, prospective reptile owners must align their individual preferences and lifestyles with the appropriate reptile species. This critical step ensures that both the reptile and its owner enjoy a harmonious and mutually beneficial relationship. Factors to consider include the reptile's activity level, spatial and enclosure requirements, the desired extent of human interaction, any allergies affecting the owner or household members, noise tolerance, time availability for feeding, cleaning, and maintenance, personal aesthetic preferences, and adherence to local legal regulations.

Ultimately, the welfare of the reptile should always remain paramount. Reptile ownership constitutes a long-term commitment, and responsible ownership entails meticulous planning and dedicated care to meet the specific needs of the scaly companion. Each reptile species possesses a unique set of characteristics, and with the appropriate level of care and attention, they can evolve into captivating and cherished companions for their owners.

Legal and Ethical Aspects of Reptile Ownership

Caring for reptiles as pets offers a fascinating and unique experience, but it also involves adherence to various rules and ethical considerations that can differ depending on one's location. These rules and ethical principles are vital to ensure the well-being of reptiles and the safety of their human caretakers.

Legal Requirements for Keeping Reptiles in Different Regions:

Reptile ownership is subject to a patchwork of laws and regulations that vary from one region to another. These regulations are designed to strike a balance between safeguarding the welfare of reptiles and ensuring public safety. One of the fundamental aspects of these legal requirements involves species-specific restrictions, permits, and guidelines tailored to govern the ownership and care of reptiles.

These species-specific restrictions aim to manage the ownership of certain reptile species based on factors such as their potential danger, conservation status, or potential for becoming invasive in local environments. For example, regions often have stringent regulations or even bans on the ownership of venomous snakes and large constrictors due to the associated risks.

Permits and licenses play a crucial role in regulating reptile ownership. In many areas, reptile owners may need to obtain specific permits or licenses to keep certain species. These permits often come with specific conditions, which may include periodic inspections of enclosures, demonstrating expertise in reptile care, or adhering to defined care standards. The goal is to ensure that reptiles are housed and cared for in a manner that guarantees their welfare.

Another important legal aspect is record-keeping. Many regions require reptile owners to maintain detailed records of their reptiles, including information on acquisition and disposition. These records serve multiple purposes, including monitoring reptile populations, ensuring compliance with legal regulations, and aiding in conservation efforts.

The transport and trade of reptiles across borders are subject to international regulations aimed at preventing illegal wildlife trafficking. The Convention on International Trade in Endangered Species of Wild Fauna and Flora

(CITES) is a significant international treaty that plays a central role in monitoring and controlling the international trade of endangered reptile species. CITES categorizes species into different appendices based on their conservation status, with strict regulations and permit requirements for species listed in Appendix I, which includes those facing the highest risk of extinction.

Ethical Considerations in Reptile Breeding and Trade:

Ethical considerations play a crucial role in reptile breeding and trade, focusing on the welfare of reptiles, preventing harm to wild populations, and promoting responsible practices within the reptile community.

Ethical breeding practices prioritize the health and well-being of the animals involved. This includes ensuring that parent reptiles are healthy and not subject to undue stress. Ethical breeders refrain from excessive breeding for profit and avoid practices that could lead to inbreeding.

A pivotal ethical choice in reptile ownership is the decision between acquiring wild-caught or captive-bred specimens.

Captive breeding is generally considered more ethical as it helps reduce pressure on wild populations and minimizes the stress and harm that can occur during the capture and transportation of wild reptiles. Supporting captive breeding programs contributes to the conservation of reptiles by reducing the demand for wild-caught individuals.

Transparency and accurate documentation are ethical

imperatives in the reptile trade. Reptile sellers should provide prospective buyers with precise information about the species they are offering, including details about the reptile's origin, care requirements, and specific needs. Transparent transactions help prevent uninformed purchases and promote responsible reptile ownership.

Reptile owners and breeders also have an ethical duty to raise awareness about reptile conservation. Education plays a pivotal role in fostering a conservation mindset within the reptile community and the general public. By sharing knowledge about reptiles and their conservation needs, enthusiasts can contribute to the preservation of these remarkable creatures and their habitats.

Reptile welfare is a cornerstone of ethical reptile ownership. Prioritizing the physical and psychological well-being of reptiles through proper enclosure design, diet, healthcare, and enrichment is essential. Ethical reptile owners provide an environment that allows their reptiles to express natural behaviors and thrive.

Promoting Sustainable Practices and Conservation Awareness:

Promoting sustainability and conservation awareness within the reptile community is vital for the long-term well-being of reptile species and their ecosystems.

Supporting conservation organizations dedicated to reptile conservation and research is a meaningful way to contribute to the protection of endangered reptile species and their habitats.

These organizations often work tirelessly to ensure the survival of reptile populations in the wild. Educational outreach is another powerful tool for raising awareness about reptile conservation. Sharing knowledge about the importance of preserving natural habitats, supporting conservation initiatives, and engaging in responsible practices in the reptile pet trade are all ways in which enthusiasts can make a meaningful difference.

Taking care of the places where reptiles live in the wild is also crucial. Responsible reptile owners recognize the importance of preserving natural habitats. This means avoiding harm to the environment and ensuring that reptiles have a safe and healthy home.

In conclusion, responsible reptile ownership involves not only the proper care of these captivating creatures but also adherence to legal requirements and ethical considerations. Understanding regional laws, breeding ethics, and the impact of the reptile trade on wild populations is essential.

By promoting sustainable practices and conservation awareness, reptile owners can actively contribute to the preservation of these remarkable creatures and their natural habitats, ensuring a brighter future for reptiles and reptile enthusiasts alike.

Chapter 2

Setting Up the Perfect Enclosure

Setting up the perfect enclosure for your reptile is essential to ensure their well-being and happiness. The enclosure serves as their home, providing them with the right environment to thrive.

Types of Enclosures

When it comes to providing a suitable home for your reptile companion, choosing the right type of enclosure is crucial.

Different reptile species have varying habitat requirements, and selecting the appropriate enclosure can significantly impact their well-being. In this section, we will delve into the various types of enclosures, such as vivarium, terrariums, and others, examining their advantages, disadvantages, and how they can be customized to cater to the needs of different reptile species.

Vivariums

Vivariums are specialized enclosures designed to

mimic a specific natural habitat. They often incorporate living plants, providing a more natural and biologically diverse environment for reptiles. Vivariums come in various sizes and can be customized to meet the specific needs of your reptile.

Advantages

One of the primary advantages of vivarium is their ability to recreate a natural environment. The inclusion of live plants not only enhances aesthetics but also contributes to improved air quality as plants help filter toxins and maintain humidity levels. Vivarium are ideal for reptile species that thrive in lush, tropical settings.

Disadvantages

Vivarium require more maintenance, as live plants need care and attention. Achieving the right balance of light, temperature, and humidity can be challenging, and overgrowth of plants can obscure the reptile's visibility. Additionally, vivarium can be more expensive to set up initially.

Customization

Customizing a vivarium involves selecting appropriate plant species that match the reptile's natural habitat. Adding branches, rocks, and hides can create a more naturalistic and stimulating environment. Proper lighting and humidity control are essential to maintain a healthy ecosystem within the vivarium.

Terrariums

Terrariums are perhaps the most common type of reptile enclosure. They are typically glass or acrylic containers with a solid base, making them suitable for reptiles that do not require high humidity levels or elaborate environments.

Advantages

Terrariums offer excellent visibility of the reptile and are relatively easy to clean and maintain. They are suitable for a wide range of reptile species, including desert-dwelling reptiles.

Disadvantages

While versatile, terrariums may not be the best choice for reptile species that require high humidity or those that need an enriched environment with live plants. Limited space and reduced airflow can also be constraints for certain species.

Customization

Customizing a terrarium involves selecting appropriate substrates, decorations, and temperature control elements based on the specific requirements of your reptile. Desert species may need sand or reptile-safe soil, while hides and basking areas are essential for most reptiles.

Aquariums

Aquariums are typically designed for fish, but they can also serve as enclosures for semi-aquatic reptiles, such as turtles and some amphibians. These enclosures feature a water section and a dry land area.

Advantages

Aquariums provide a clear view of the reptile, making it easy to observe their behavior. They are well-suited for semi-aquatic species and offer the opportunity to create aquatic and terrestrial environments within one enclosure.

Disadvantages

Maintaining water quality in the aquatic portion can be challenging, requiring filtration and regular water changes. Additionally, aquariums may not be ideal for fully terrestrial reptiles.

Customization

Customizing an aquarium involves creating a suitable land area with appropriate substrate and hiding spots. The aquatic section should have proper filtration and heating elements to maintain water quality and temperature.

Screen Cages

Screen cages are made of mesh or wire, providing excellent ventilation and airflow. They are commonly used for arboreal reptile species that require high humidity levels.

Advantages

Screen cages offer superior ventilation, which is crucial for reptiles that need fresh air. They are also lightweight and easy to clean. The open design allows for the installation of climbing structures and foliage.

Disadvantages

Screen cages may not retain heat and humidity as effectively as glass or plastic enclosures. For reptiles that require high humidity, additional efforts are needed to maintain the right conditions. Escaping insects or small reptiles can also be a concern.

Customization

Customizing a screen cage involves selecting suitable substrates, branches, and foliage for arboreal reptiles. Maintaining humidity can be achieved through misting systems, humidifiers, or by covering parts of the cage with plastic or glass.

Racks and Tubs

Racks and tubs are often used for breeding and housing multiple reptiles in a compact space. They are stackable and space efficient.

Advantages

Racks and tubs are space-saving solutions for breeders

or enthusiasts with multiple reptiles. They provide a controlled environment and are easy to maintain.

Disadvantages

These enclosures may not be visually appealing and lack the aesthetic qualities of vivarium or terrariums. They are typically used for breeding or quarantine purposes and may not offer the same level of environmental enrichment.

Customization

Customizing racks and tubs involves selecting appropriate tub sizes, substrates, and heat sources. While not as visually stimulating, they can still provide a comfortable and controlled environment for reptiles.

Choosing the right type of enclosure for your reptile involves careful consideration of the species' specific requirements. Each type of enclosure has its advantages and disadvantages, and customization is key to meeting the unique needs of your scaly companion. Providing a suitable and comfortable environment is essential for the health and happiness of your reptile.

Size and Design Considerations for Reptile Enclosures

Creating an ideal living space for your reptile involves careful consideration of both size and design. The size of the enclosure directly impacts the reptile's comfort and wellbeing, while the design plays a crucial role in providing environmental enrichment and mimicking their natural habitat. In this section, we will delve into the guidelines for calculating optimal enclosure size, the importance of environmental enrichment in design, and explore case studies of well-designed reptile enclosures.

Calculating Optimal Enclosure Size

Determining the right enclosure size for your reptile is a critical step in ensuring their health and happiness. The enclosure size should reflect the species' natural behaviors, activity level, and growth potential. A general rule of thumb is that the enclosure should be as large as your space and budget allows.

When determining the optimal size of your reptile's enclosure, several considerations come into play. The floor space of the enclosure is a critical factor, ensuring that your reptile has sufficient room to engage in natural behaviors comfortably. For terrestrial reptiles, the enclosure should be generously sized, typically at least double the length of the reptile. Conversely, for arboreal species like chameleons and tree-dwelling snakes, the height of the enclosure is of paramount importance, often matching or exceeding the length of the reptile to accommodate their climbing and perching behaviors.

Additionally, it's essential to consider your reptile's growth potential. Reptiles can vary significantly in size as they mature, and planning for their future size is more cost effective and less stressful than frequent enclosure upgrades. Ensuring that the enclosure accommodates their adult dimensions is crucial to their long-term wellbeing.

The activity level of your reptile is another crucial factor to consider when determining enclosure size. Active reptiles, such as monitors or certain lizard species, require more extensive enclosures to facilitate movement, exploration, and exercise.

Providing ample room for physical activity is vital for their overall health and mental stimulation.

Furthermore, species-specific guidelines should be considered when designing the enclosure. Different reptile species may have unique requirements in terms of space and design. For example, some snake species may thrive in tubular enclosures that mimic their natural burrowing tendencies, while others may need a more open and spacious environment to accommodate their behaviors and preferences.

Importance of Environmental Enrichment in Design

Environmental enrichment is essential for reptiles as it stimulates their physical and mental well-being. A well-designed enclosure should offer a dynamic and engaging environment that encourages natural behaviors.

Hiding spots are crucial components of reptile enclosures. These spots provide reptiles with a safe retreat when they feel stressed or need to thermoregulate. Proper placement of hiding spots throughout the enclosure ensures that reptiles have access to these safe spaces whenever necessary.

For arboreal species like chameleons and tree-dwelling snakes, providing climbing opportunities is vital. This can be achieved by incorporating branches, vines, and climbing structures within the enclosure. These elements not only encourage exercise but also enable reptiles to exhibit their natural behaviors, leading to a more enriched and fulfilling life in captivity.

A designated basking area with appropriate temperature gradients is essential. Many reptiles require access to a basking spot to regulate their body temperature effectively. This area should offer a range of temperatures, allowing reptiles to choose the optimal spot for thermoregulation.

The choice of substrate within the enclosure should align with the reptile's natural habitat. Different species may thrive with specific substrates, which can include options like sand, coconut fiber, cypress mulch, or even paper towels. Selecting the right substrate ensures a comfortable and authentic environment for the reptile.

Adding natural elements such as rocks, logs, and other visually stimulating decorations can significantly enhance the enclosure's overall environment. These elements serve dual purposes—they provide opportunities for exploration as reptiles navigate their surroundings, and they offer hiding spots that contribute to their sense of security.

Adequate lighting is crucial for the health of many reptiles, especially those that require UVB lighting. UVB lighting facilitates calcium absorption, mimicking the benefits of natural sunlight. Proper lighting setups ensure that reptiles receive the essential UVB rays they need to thrive in captivity.

Incorporating feeding strategies that encourage hunting

and foraging behaviors is an essential aspect of environmental enrichment. This can involve hiding prey within the enclosure, using puzzle feeders, or implementing other techniques that require reptiles to actively seek out their food. These strategies not only stimulate their mental faculties but also contribute to a more engaged and fulfilled life.

Substrate Options and Their Roles in Reptile Enclosures

The choice of substrate is a critical aspect of designing a reptile enclosure, as it plays a multifaceted role in creating a suitable and comfortable environment for captive reptiles. Different substrates serve various functions, impacting humidity levels, cleanliness, and the overall well-being of the reptiles. In this discussion, we'll examine various substrate options, their roles, and practical tips for cleaning and maintenance.

Sand

Sand is a popular substrate choice for reptile keepers, particularly for desert-dwelling species like bearded dragons and certain geckos. Its fine texture allows for easy digging and burrowing, which many reptiles find stimulating. Sand also offers a natural appearance, enhancing the aesthetics of the enclosure.

However, sand can pose challenges in terms of humidity control. It tends to absorb moisture slowly, making it less suitable for species that require higher humidity levels. Moreover, fine sand can be accidentally ingested by reptiles during feeding, potentially leading to impaction—a serious health concern. To mitigate these risks, some keepers mix sand with other substrates or opt for alternative materials.

Coconut Coir

Coconut coir, derived from coconut husks, is a substrate gaining popularity due to its versatility and moisture-retaining properties. It provides a soft and comfortable surface for reptiles to walk on and allows for natural burrowing behaviors.

One of coconut coir's primary advantages is its ability to maintain humidity levels. It retains moisture well, making it an excellent choice for species requiring higher humidity, such as certain snakes and amphibians. Keepers often mix coconut coir with water to create a moist substrate layer that aids in shedding and promotes hydration.

Cypress Mulch

Cypress mulch is a substrate commonly used for various reptile species, including snakes and lizards. It offers a natural appearance and texture, making it aesthetically pleasing. Cypress mulch is available in different sizes, allowing keepers to choose a suitable texture for their reptiles.

One of the roles of cypress mulch is in helping to maintain humidity levels. It holds moisture effectively and slowly releases it, creating a stable and suitable environment for reptiles that require moderate humidity. Additionally, cypress mulch provides insulation, assisting in regulating temperature within the enclosure.

Newspaper/Paper Towels

For some reptile keepers, simplicity and ease of cleaning are priorities. Newspaper or paper towels are minimalist substrate choices that make enclosure maintenance straightforward. They are affordable and readily available, making them convenient for temporary enclosures or quarantine setups.

While newspaper and paper towels excel in cleanliness, they lack the natural aesthetics and opportunities for burrowing that other substrates offer. They are most suitable for reptiles with low substrate requirements, such as certain snakes or hospital enclosures where cleanliness is paramount.

Cleaning and Maintenance

Maintaining a clean and hygienic reptile enclosure is essential for the well-being of your scaly companions. Proper cleaning and maintenance practices help ensure a safe and healthy environment. Here are some key considerations:

Regular spot cleaning is a fundamental aspect of enclosure maintenance. It involves removing waste and soiled substrate from the enclosure on a daily or as-needed basis. Reptile waste can accumulate quickly and, if left unattended, may lead to hygiene issues and unpleasant odours.

Depending on the type of substrate used, consider replacing a portion of it periodically. For substrates like sand or coconut coir, it's advisable to replace about one-third of the substrate every few months. This helps maintain cleanliness and prevent the buildup of waste and bacteria.

In some cases, a complete substrate change may be necessary. This becomes essential if the substrate becomes excessively soiled, contaminated with parasites, or shows signs of Mold growth. When conducting a complete substrate change, thoroughly clean and disinfect the enclosure and all associated equipment.

Disinfection is a critical step when cleaning the enclosure and handling substrate. Use reptile-safe disinfectants to clean surfaces, furnishings, and any equipment used in the enclosure. Proper disinfection helps prevent the spread of pathogens and keeps your reptiles healthy.

Regularly monitor the humidity levels within the enclosure, especially if you are using substrates that significantly impact humidity. Adjustments may be needed to maintain the optimal humidity range for your specific reptile species. Inadequate or excessive humidity can lead to health issues, such as respiratory problems or improper shedding.

In addition to routine cleaning, pay close attention to your reptile's behavior and overall health. Changes in behavior, appetite, or shedding patterns can be indicators of potential issues with the enclosure or substrate. Regular health checks are essential to catch any problems early and address them promptly.

Temperature and Humidity Control in Reptile Enclosures

Maintaining appropriate temperature and humidity levels within a reptile enclosure is paramount to the health and well-being of captive reptiles. Understanding the concepts of temperature gradients, advanced temperature control methods, and managing humidity fluctuations are essential aspects of responsible reptile ownership.

Temperature Gradients

Creating temperature gradients within the enclosure is a fundamental practice in reptile husbandry. Temperature gradients mimic the natural conditions reptiles encounter in the wild, allowing them to regulate their body temperature effectively.

In simplest terms, a temperature gradient means having a range of temperatures within the enclosure. This typically includes a warmer basking area and a cooler, shaded area. For diurnal reptiles, like many lizards, the basking spot should provide a higher temperature than the cooler zone. Nocturnal reptiles, on the other hand, may require a different setup, with a warm hiding spot and a cooler area for rest.

Temperature gradients enable reptiles to thermoregulate by moving between warmer and cooler areas as needed. This behavior is essential for digestion, metabolism, and overall health.

Advanced Methods for Precise Temperature Control

Precise temperature control may be necessary for some reptile species with specific temperature requirements. Several advanced methods are available to achieve this level of control.

One effective method involves using heat mats and cables, which can be strategically placed beneath or within the enclosure substrate to create localized heating zones. These are particularly useful for reptiles that require consistent belly heat, such as snakes. The warmth generated by these mats and cables mimics the reptile's natural environment, ensuring their comfort and wellbeing.

Ceramic heat emitters are specialized heat-producing bulbs that emit infrared heat without emitting visible light. These emitters are suitable for providing ambient warmth within the enclosure without disrupting the reptile's day-night cycle. They are especially beneficial for reptiles that require a steady and gentle source of heat to maintain their desired temperature range.

The use of thermostats is considered essential when it comes to maintaining accurate and stable temperatures within a reptile enclosure. These devices allow for precise control of heating elements, ensuring that temperatures remain within the desired range. Thermostats effectively prevent temperature fluctuations, providing a consistent and comfortable environment for the reptiles.

Radiant heat panels offer an efficient heating solution that distributes warmth evenly across the entire enclosure. This method is particularly advantageous for larger enclosures or reptiles that require a constant and widespread heat source. Radiant heat panels ensure that every corner of the enclosure remains at the optimal temperature, promoting the reptile's overall well-being.

Specialized halogen or tungsten bulbs are capable of

emitting intense heat. These bulbs are often used to create concentrated basking areas within the enclosure. Reptiles that require high-temperature basking spots, such as certain species of lizards, benefit from the intense heat generated by these bulbs. These bulbs help replicate the reptile's natural behavior of thermoregulation by providing a warm and comfortable basking area.

Understanding and managing humidity fluctuations

Humidity control is another critical aspect of reptile care, as different species have varying humidity requirements. Effective management of humidity levels can be achieved through several methods.

One crucial factor in humidity control is substrate selection. Different substrates have different moisture-retaining properties. Substrates like coconut coir and cypress mulch are excellent choices for retaining moisture, making them suitable for reptiles that require higher humidity levels. In contrast, substrates like sand may not be the best option for species with more stringent humidity needs.

Misting systems, as well as regular manual misting, are effective ways to increase humidity levels within the enclosure. These methods are particularly important for reptiles originating from tropical or humid regions. By providing a fine mist, keepers can elevate and maintain the necessary humidity, promoting the well-being of their reptilian companions.

In certain cases, especially for larger enclosures or reptiles with strict humidity requirements, employing a humidifier may be necessary. Humidifiers can maintain consistent and optimal humidity levels within the enclosure, ensuring that the reptiles have the ideal environment to thrive.

To accurately monitor and adjust humidity levels, the use of hygrometers is indispensable. These instruments provide precise measurements of humidity within the enclosure, allowing reptile keepers to fine-tune their humidity management strategies based on the specific needs of their reptile species.

Proper ventilation is a crucial aspect of humidity control. Adequate air exchange helps prevent excessive humidity and the growth of Mold within the enclosure. Properly designed ventilation systems maintain a healthy balance of humidity while ensuring the reptiles receive the fresh air they require.

Chapter 3

Reptile Nutrition and Diet

Reptile nutrition is a crucial aspect of responsible reptile ownership. Understanding the dietary requirements of your scaly companion is essential to ensure their health and well-being. In this chapter, we will delve into the species-specific dietary needs of popular reptile species, analyse the nutritional content of common feeder insects, and explore the factors influencing dietary preferences in reptiles.

Species-Specific Dietary Requirements

Detailed dietary needs of popular reptile species.

Bearded Dragons

Bearded dragons, known for their friendly demeanor, are omnivorous reptiles with diverse dietary requirements. A significant portion of their diet comprises insects, which provide essential nutrients like protein and minerals. Among the commonly offered insects are crickets, dubia roaches, mealworms, and superworms. Each insect type offers distinct nutritional advantages and considerations for your bearded dragon's health.

Crickets are a popular staple in a bearded dragon's diet

due to their moderate to high protein content, which is important for growth and muscle maintenance. They also have a decent calcium-phosphorus ratio, making them suitable as part of a balanced diet. While crickets have moderate chitin levels, they are more digestible than mealworms.

Dubia roaches, along with other roach species, are considered one of the most nutritionally balanced insect choices. They retain a substantial amount of nutrients from their diet for up to a week before being consumed. These roaches are rich in protein and calcium, promoting muscle growth and strong bones. Additionally, they have lower chitin levels compared to mealworms, making them easier to digest and less likely to cause impaction.

Mealworms and superworms contain moderate to high protein levels, making them suitable as occasional treats. However, they have higher chitin content, which can be harder for bearded dragons to digest in excess. Therefore, they should be offered in moderation to avoid potential digestive issues.

Variety is essential, so consider offering a mix of these insects to ensure your bearded dragon receives a well-rounded diet and essential nutrients for optimal health. Always remember to dust insects with a calcium supplement to meet calcium requirements.

Additionally, bearded dragons need a variety of leafy greens, including collard greens, mustard greens, and dandelion greens, which are rich in vitamins and minerals. Vegetables like carrots, bell peppers, and squash can also be incorporated to provide additional nutrients. However, it's important to be cautious about certain vegetables that should be fed sparingly or in moderation. For instance, vegetables like spinach greens should be avoided due to their high oxalate content, which can hinder calcium absorption and potentially lead to health issues. Similarly, beets are another vegetable that should be fed in moderation as they are relatively high in sugar content. It's crucial to strike a balance in your bearded dragon's diet to ensure they receive the right mix of nutrients for their overall well-being. While fruits like strawberries, blueberries, and apples can be offered occasionally as treats, they should not make up a significant part of their diet due to their sugar content. Also, citrus should not be used as it causes gout.

Dusting insects and vegetables with calcium powder and providing vitamin supplements is crucial to prevent nutritional deficiencies and ensure overall health.

Ball Pythons

All snakes can be fed frozen-thawed rodents, but it is

crucial to ensure they are fully thawed to avoid endangering the reptile and causing problems with maintaining their blood temperatures, which can ultimately lead to the snake's death.

Ball pythons, unlike some other reptiles, are strict carnivores. In captivity, their diet primarily consists of appropriately sized rodents, such as mice and rats. It's essential to choose prey items that match the snake's girth to ensure they can be safely consumed and digested. The size of the prey is a critical consideration in the diet of ball pythons to promote their health and well-being.

Red-Eared Sliders

Red-eared sliders are aquatic turtles with a diet that spans both animal and plant matter. Their dietary requirements are diverse and include commercial turtle pellets, which provide essential nutrients and can serve as a staple of their diet. In addition to pellets, they also need a variety of aquatic plants like duckweed and water lettuce. Occasional protein sources such as insects and small fish can be included in their diet. Leafy greens like kale and collard greens should be offered for fiber and additional vitamins. Maintaining a balanced diet is crucial to support their overall well-being.

Leopard Geckos

Leopard geckos are insectivores with straightforward dietary needs. Their diet mainly consists of insects such as crickets, dubia roaches, and mealworms. When selecting the insects to feed your leopard gecko, it's crucial to ensure that they are around the same size as their eye span, which matches the gecko's age and size. Offering a variety of insects ensures they receive a well-rounded diet rich in essential nutrients.

Corn Snakes

Corn snakes are carnivorous snakes with specific dietary preferences. In captivity, they primarily consume appropriately sized rodents like mice. The size of the prey should correspond to the snake's widest portion to ensure safe consumption and digestion. Properly meeting their dietary needs by providing correctly sized rodents is essential for their overall health and well-being.

Russian Tortoises

Russian tortoises are herbivorous reptiles with a plant-based diet. They primarily consume a variety of leafy greens, including endive, escarole, and chicory. Additionally, offering vegetables like carrots, bell peppers, and zucchini provides dietary variety and additional nutrients. Occasional fruits like strawberries and apples can be given as treats, but they should not be a significant part of their diet and make sure not to add citrus as it causes gout. Ensuring a balanced diet rich in fiber and calcium is essential for their health.

Green Iguanas

Green iguanas are primarily herbivores, with their diet mainly consisting of leafy greens such as collard greens, mustard greens, and turnip greens. Offering a variety of leafy greens ensures they receive essential nutrients. Additionally, providing vegetables like squash, sweet potatoes, and bell peppers adds variety to their diet. While primarily herbivorous, young green iguanas may occasionally eat insects, but this should be limited. Properly meeting their dietary requirements helps maintain their health and well-being.

Factors influencing dietary preferences in reptiles

Analysing the nutritional content of common feeder insects is a vital aspect of reptile nutrition. Feeder insects serve as a primary source of protein for many reptile species, and understanding their nutritional value is essential to provide a well-balanced diet.

Common feeder insects include crickets, dubia roaches, mealworms, and superworms, each offering varying nutritional benefits. Crickets, for example, are rich in protein and calcium, making them an excellent choice for reptiles that require high protein intake and calcium supplementation. On the other hand, dubia roaches are known for their low-fat content and high protein levels, making them a suitable choice for reptiles with specific dietary needs.

Mealworms and superworms are popular choices, but they are higher in fat compared to crickets and dubia roaches. While they can be part of a reptile's diet, moderation is crucial to prevent excessive fat intake, which can lead to obesity and related health issues.

Aside from the nutritional content of feeder insects, factors influencing dietary preferences in reptiles are equally important to consider. These factors can help reptile owners better understand their pets' feeding behaviors and tailor their diets accordingly.

Natural Habitat

Reptiles often exhibit dietary preferences that align with their natural habitats. For instance, species originating from arid regions may have adapted to a diet of insects and arthropods found in their environment, while those from lush tropical areas may consume a variety of fruits and plant matter.

Age and Life Stage

The dietary preferences of reptiles may change as they age and grow. Young reptiles often require higher protein intake for growth and development, while adults may transition to a more herbivorous diet or maintain a consistent diet throughout their lives.

Health and Medical Conditions

Some reptiles may develop dietary preferences due to underlying health conditions or medical issues. For example, a reptile with dental problems may prefer softer food items, while reptiles recovering from illnesses may require a specific diet to aid in their recovery.

Environmental Factors

The environment in which a reptile is housed can impact its dietary preferences. Factors such as temperature, humidity, and lighting play a role in a reptile's appetite and digestion. Maintaining appropriate environmental conditions can help regulate their feeding behaviors.

Social Behavior

In certain cases, social interactions with other reptiles may influence dietary preferences. For example, reptiles that are kept in groups may observe and mimic the feeding behaviors of their companions.

Individual Variation

Just like humans, reptiles have individual preferences. Two reptiles of the same species may have different tastes and preferences when it comes to their food. It's essential to consider the unique preferences of each reptile and offer a variety of food items to accommodate their choices.

Acquired Preferences

Reptiles can develop acquired preferences based on their previous diet and experiences. For example, if a captive reptile has been consistently fed a particular type of prey item, it may develop a preference for that item.

Understanding these factors and closely observing your reptile's behavior and preferences can help you tailor their diet to meet their specific needs. Providing a diverse range of food items and ensuring a balanced diet is essential for the overall health and wellbeing of your scaly companion.

Feeding Schedules

Feeding schedules are a crucial aspect of reptile care that can significantly impact the health and well-being of these scaly companions. Tailoring feeding routines to accommodate factors such as the reptile's age, fasting periods, and individual health and activity levels is essential for their overall health and vitality.

Age-Specific Feeding Schedules

One of the fundamental considerations when establishing a feeding schedule for reptiles is their age. Reptiles undergo distinct stages of growth and development, each with its specific dietary requirements.

For hatchlings and juveniles, which are in the early stages of growth, a more frequent feeding schedule is often necessary to support their rapid development. Young reptiles may require daily or every other day feedings to ensure they receive adequate nutrients for their growth. Providing a diverse range of small, nutritious prey items or suitable commercial diets is vital during this phase to meet their nutritional needs.

As reptiles mature into the subadult stage, their growth rate typically slows down. Consequently, feeding frequency can be gradually reduced to every few days or even weekly, depending on the species. Monitoring their growth and adjusting the feeding schedule accordingly is crucial to prevent overfeeding, which can lead to obesity and associated health issues.

In adulthood, reptiles have generally reached their full size and growth potential. Feeding schedules for adult reptiles can vary significantly among species. While some may require feeding every few days, others may thrive on a weekly or biweekly feeding schedule. The key during this stage is to provide a well-balanced diet that aligns with their nutritional needs while considering the species-specific requirements.

Accommodating Fasting Periods

Many reptiles undergo natural fasting periods as a response to environmental changes, such as temperature fluctuations and daylight hours. These fasting periods are influenced by factors such as the reptile's species, geographic origin, and natural behaviors. Reptile owners should be aware of these fasting periods and make necessary adjustments to their feeding schedules.

Seasonal fasting is common among reptiles living in temperate zones. Tortoises and some snake species are known to undergo seasonal fasting during the colder winter months when temperatures drop. This behavior is a natural response to reduced metabolic activity and decreased availability of prey. During these periods, reptiles may eat very little or not at all. It is essential to provide a stress-free environment and monitor their health to ensure they are handling seasonal fasting appropriately.

Fasting can also occur during breeding and reproduction. Female reptiles may fast as they prepare to lay eggs, and additional care and nutrition should be provided to support these reproductive processes. Calcium and vitamin supplementation may be necessary during this time to ensure the reptile's health.

Stress-induced fasting is another factor to consider. Reptiles may refuse food due to stress, illness, or changes in their environment. Identifying and addressing the underlying cause of stress is crucial to encourage normal feeding behavior. Providing a quiet and secure environment can help alleviate stress-induced fasting.

Adjusting Feeding Frequency for Individual Health and Activity Levels

Reptiles, like humans, exhibit individual variations in metabolism, activity levels, and dietary preferences. These factors should be taken into account when determining the appropriate feeding frequency for an individual reptile.

Some reptiles may have higher metabolic rates than others, leading to increased energy expenditure. Monitoring their weight and overall health can help determine if they require more frequent feedings to maintain their energy levels and nutritional needs.

The activity level of a reptile can also influence its feeding frequency. Active reptiles that spend more time exploring and moving may burn more calories and require more frequent feeding to sustain their energy levels. In contrast, sedentary reptiles may need less frequent feedings, as their energy expenditure is lower.

Health status is another critical factor to consider. Reptiles recovering from illness or injury may require more frequent, smaller meals to aid in their rehabilitation and provide the necessary nutrients for healing. Conversely, overweight reptiles may need a reduced feeding schedule to support weight loss and prevent obesity-related health issues.

Additionally, it's worth noting that some reptiles, such as ball pythons, can go for extended periods without food, sometimes up to six months, although access to water remains essential during these fasting periods. Also, certain reptiles, particularly snakes, may exhibit decreased appetite when they reach a certain size, leading to temporary fasting periods lasting a few weeks or even a month. Understanding and accommodating these natural behaviors and adjusting feeding schedules accordingly is part of responsible reptile care.

Supplements and their Importance

Supplements are a crucial component of reptile care, ensuring that these unique creatures receive the essential vitamins and minerals they require to thrive. Understanding the specific nutritional needs of reptiles, including calcium, vitamin D3, and others, is essential to prevent nutritional deficiencies and related health issues. By properly supplementing live prey and vegetables as part of their diet, reptile owners can help maintain their pets' overall health and vitality, promoting a long and fulfilling life for these remarkable animals.

Specific Vitamin and Mineral Requirements:

Reptiles, like all living creatures, have unique dietary requirements when it comes to vitamins and minerals. These essential nutrients play various roles in their overall health and physiological processes. Let's explore some of the specific requirements for reptiles:

Calcium is a fundamental mineral for reptiles, as it is essential for bone health and muscle function. Reptiles need sufficient amounts of dietary calcium to maintain strong bones and eggshell formation in egg-laying species. Inadequate calcium intake can lead to metabolic bone disease (MBD), a severe health condition characterized by weakened bones, deformities, and organ dysfunction.

Vitamin D3 is closely associated with calcium metabolism in reptiles. To absorb and utilize dietary calcium effectively, reptiles require an adequate supply of vitamin D3. This vitamin is synthesized by the reptile's skin when exposed to UVB radiation from natural sunlight or UVB lighting. Without sufficient vitamin D3, reptiles can struggle to absorb calcium, even if it is present in their diet.

Vitamin A is crucial for maintaining healthy skin, mucous membranes, and vision. Reptiles deficient in vitamin A can experience skin problems, respiratory issues, and eye abnormalities. It is essential to provide reptiles with an appropriate source of vitamin A to prevent these health issues.

Vitamin B Complex: The B vitamins are essential for various metabolic processes in reptiles, including energy production and nerve function. Reptiles can receive vitamin B from UVB lights as well as from supplements Vitamin C: While reptiles do not require vitamin C in the same way that humans do, some species may benefit from limited amounts of this vitamin. In captivity, providing a variety of fresh fruits and vegetables can help ensure they receive any necessary vitamin C.

Understanding the Role of Supplements:

Supplements are used to bridge the nutritional gaps in a reptile's diet, ensuring that they receive the necessary vitamins and minerals to maintain optimal health. The role of specific supplements, such as calcium, vitamin D3, and others, is critical to preventing nutritional deficiencies and related health issues.

Calcium supplements are essential for reptiles, particularly those with high calcium requirements, such as herbivores and egg laying species. These supplements come in different forms, including calcium carbonate and calcium gluconate. It is essential to select an appropriate calcium supplement and provide it according to the reptile's specific dietary needs. Calcium supplements should be dusted onto food items or offered in a separate dish, depending on the reptile's feeding behavior.

Vitamin D3 supplements are necessary for reptiles, especially those housed indoors or in environments with limited access to natural sunlight. Without adequate UVB exposure, reptiles cannot produce sufficient vitamin D3 on their own. Vitamin D3 supplements are typically available as a liquid or powder and can be administered orally or applied topically to the reptile's skin.

Multivitamin supplements are designed to provide a wide range of essential vitamins and minerals in one convenient form. While they can be beneficial for certain reptiles, it's essential to use them in moderation and avoid over-supplementation, as excessive intake of certain vitamins and minerals can be harmful.

Practical Advice on Supplementing Live Prey and Vegetables

Supplementing live prey and vegetables is a common practice among reptile owners to ensure their pets receive the necessary nutrients. Here are some practical guidelines for supplementing these food items:

Live Prey

When feeding live prey items to reptiles, it's essential to "dust" or coat them with the appropriate supplements before offering them to the reptile. For example, crickets or mealworms can be placed in a container with a small amount of calcium powder and shaken to coat them evenly. Ensure that the supplements adhere to the prey items and are consumed by the reptile. It's important to note that rodents do not require dusting with supplements as they have different nutritional profiles compared to insects.

Vegetables

For reptiles that consume vegetables, supplements can be sprinkled directly onto the food items. Vegetables should be washed and chopped as needed, and the supplements can be lightly dusted over the veggies before feeding. Ensure that the reptile consumes the supplemented vegetables as part of its balanced diet.

Proper Schedule

Supplements should be administered as part of a regular feeding schedule. The frequency of supplementation may vary depending on the reptile's species, age, and specific dietary requirements. It is crucial to follow recommended guidelines and consult with a veterinarian or reptile expert for guidance on supplementing your reptile.

Supplements are a crucial component of reptile care, ensuring that these unique creatures receive the essential vitamins and minerals they require to thrive. Understanding the specific nutritional needs of reptiles, including calcium, vitamin D3, and others, is essential to prevent nutritional deficiencies and related health issues. By properly supplementing live prey and vegetables as part of their diet, reptile owners can help maintain their pets' overall health and vitality, promoting a long and fulfilling life for these remarkable animals.

Chapter 4

Handling and Taming Your Reptile

Handling and taming your reptile are important aspects of responsible reptile ownership. It allows you to interact with your scaly companion, build a bond of trust, and ensure their well-being. However, it's crucial to approach this process with care and knowledge to ensure both your safety and the comfort of your reptile. In this chapter, we will explore the best practices for handling and taming various reptile species, taking into consideration their unique characteristics and individual temperaments. Whether you are a beginner or an experienced reptile owner, understanding how to handle and tame your reptile is key to fostering a positive and enriching relationship with these fascinating creatures.

Safe Handling Techniques

Step-by-step guide to safely pick up and handle different reptiles

Handling reptiles is an exciting and rewarding aspect

of keeping them as pets or working with them in a professional capacity. However, it's crucial to approach handling with care and knowledge to ensure the wellbeing of both the reptile and the handler. This comprehensive guide will provide essential tips and techniques for safely picking up and handling different types of reptiles.

Before attempting to handle any reptile, it's essential to conduct thorough research about the specific species you'll be working with. Different reptiles have varying temperaments, behaviors, and handling requirements. Understanding their natural habitat, feeding habits, and potential defensive mechanisms will help you approach handling with confidence.

Cleanliness is vital when handling reptiles. Always wash your hands thoroughly before and after handling to reduce the risk of transmitting bacteria or pathogens between you and the reptile. This practice also minimizes the chances of infection for both you and the reptile.

Reptiles can be sensitive to sudden movements and loud noises. Approach the reptile slowly and calmly to avoid startling or stressing it. Avoid fast, erratic movements, which can trigger a defensive response.

Depending on the size and species of the reptile, consider using appropriate handling tools or equipment. For smaller reptiles like geckos or small snakes, clean, dry hands may suffice. For larger or potentially more aggressive reptiles, specialized handling tools such as snake hooks or gentle graspers can provide added control and safety.

When picking up a reptile, it's crucial to provide proper

support for its body. This helps prevent injury to the reptile and promotes a sense of security. For example:

Snakes should be supported along their length, with one hand at the front and another near the tail if necessary.

Lizards can be gently scooped up, ensuring that their legs are well-supported and not dangling.

Refrain from squeezing or applying excessive pressure on the reptile, as this can cause discomfort or harm. Use gentle, controlled handling techniques, especially around sensitive areas like the abdomen or chest.

Many reptiles have natural defensive behaviors, such as hissing, puffing up, or attempting to bite when they feel threatened. If a reptile exhibits defensive behavior, it's essential to remain calm and patient. Give the reptile time to acclimate to your touch and handle it gently and confidently.

Reptiles are ectothermic, meaning they rely on external sources of heat to regulate their body temperature. Ensure that the handling area is appropriately warm, as reptiles can become stressed in cold environments. Avoid extended handling sessions in colder conditions.

Minimize the duration of handling sessions, especially for species that are prone to stress. Short, positive interactions are preferable to extended handling, which can lead to increased stress for the reptile.

After handling, gently and carefully return the reptile to its enclosure or habitat. Allow it time to recover and relax without further disturbance. Ensure that the enclosure provides the necessary temperature, humidity, and security to support the reptile's well-being.

Techniques for handling larger and potentially aggressive species

Handling larger and potentially aggressive reptile species demands specialized techniques and precautions to ensure the safety of both the handler and the animal. These reptiles, due to their size or temperament, may pose unique challenges that require a tailored approach. In this comprehensive guide, we will explore the strategies and principles for safely handling these fascinating but potentially formidable creatures.

Before diving into specific techniques, it is essential to comprehend the factors that can incite aggression in reptiles. Aggression is often a reaction to perceived threats or stressors, and recognizing these triggers is crucial:

Feeling cornered or trapped can provoke defensive behavior.

Aggression in reptiles can be triggered by various factors, including the protection of territory, resources such as food or mates, hormonal changes during breeding seasons, or underlying health issues. Identifying these triggers in the specific reptile species you are handling is crucial for anticipating and effectively mitigating potential risks. The timing of your interactions also plays a significant role in safe handling. Avoid handling reptiles during periods of stress or heightened aggression, considering factors such as the time of day when some reptiles are more active and responsive, the proximity to feeding times that may make them perceive your presence as a threat to their meal, and the mating season when territorial or aggressive behaviors can be more pronounced.

Appropriate handling tools can provide an added layer of safety when dealing with larger or potentially aggressive reptiles. Commonly used tools include snake hooks, gentle graspers, and shields or barriers. These tools allow you to maintain a safer distance and reduce the risk of injury.

When approaching these reptiles, it is vital to do so slowly and cautiously. Sudden movements or loud noises can startle or agitate them, potentially leading to defensive behaviors. Maintain a respectful distance until you are confident that it is safe to proceed with the handling.

Stress can worsen aggressive behavior in reptiles, so it is crucial to minimize stress during handling. Keep the duration of handling sessions brief, provide a quiet and calm environment, and ensure that the reptile has a secure and comfortable enclosure to retreat to after handling.

Properly supporting the reptile's body is essential to prevent injury to both you and the animal. Depending on the reptile's size and anatomy, use both hands to support its body evenly. Avoid applying excessive pressure or squeezing, which can cause discomfort. Ensuring that the reptile's weight is adequately supported prevents it from dangling or feeling unstable.

Handling venomous reptiles is a practice that should be avoided, even for experienced reptile enthusiasts, due to the inherent dangers involved. Venomous reptiles, such as venomous snakes, possess potent toxins that can cause severe harm or even be fatal to humans. These toxins can lead to a range of symptoms, including tissue damage, severe pain, paralysis, and organ failure. Despite an individual's level of experience, the risk associated with handling venomous reptiles remains high, and even a single bite can have dire consequences. Therefore, it is strongly recommended that only trained professionals with the necessary knowledge and equipment should handle venomous reptiles in controlled environments, such as zoos or research facilities, where safety protocols are in place to minimize the risks associated with these animals. For the general public, observing venomous reptiles in the wild or in professionally managed settings is the safest and most responsible way to appreciate these fascinating creatures.

In situations involving larger or potentially aggressive reptiles, having a second handler can significantly enhance safety. The second handler can aid with restraining or guiding the reptile, especially if it becomes agitated or attempts to escape.

Maintaining a calm and confident demeanor during handling is paramount. Reptiles can detect fear or anxiety in their handlers, which may escalate their stress or aggression. Remaining composed and self-assured can help reassure the reptile and prevent further agitation.

In many cases, larger reptiles can be trained and socialized to reduce aggression and improve handling experiences. This process typically involves positive reinforcement techniques to associate handling with positive outcomes. However, training should only be undertaken by experienced individuals and with the guidance of experts.

Ultimately, if handling larger and potentially aggressive reptile species raises concerns about safety or if the reptile consistently displays aggressive behavior, seeking assistance from a professional reptile handler, veterinarian, or herpetologist is highly advisable. These experts can offer guidance, training, and expertise to ensure the safety of both the handler and the reptile.

Handling larger and potentially aggressive reptile species demands careful preparation, knowledge of the species' behavior, and the use of appropriate techniques and tools. Safety should always be the primary consideration, and individuals handling these reptiles should be well-trained and experienced. With the right precautions and approach, it is possible to safely interact with these magnificent creatures while minimizing stress and potential risks.

The importance of minimal stress during handling

The significance of minimizing stress during the handling of reptiles is paramount, with far-reaching implications for both the well-being of the animals and the safety of the handlers. This comprehensive exploration delves into the crucial nature of stress reduction during handling, the telltale signs of stress in reptiles, and effective strategies to ensure a low-stress experience for both the handler and the reptile.

Stress, when unchecked, can have severe consequences for the health and immunity of reptiles. It leaves them vulnerable to infections and diseases due to a compromised immune system. This is particularly concerning for captive reptiles, as they are already exposed to various stressors in their environment. Beyond physical health, stress can manifest in behavioral changes, turning once docile reptiles into aggressive or defensive creatures. These altered behaviors not only affect their quality of life but can also pose challenges and potential dangers during handling.

Furthermore, stress can wreak havoc on the digestive system of reptiles, leading to issues like regurgitation, indigestion, or even anorexia. Prolonged stress can result in malnutrition and an overall decline in health, further emphasizing the importance of minimizing stress during handling.

Recognizing the signs of stress in reptiles is the first step in addressing the issue effectively. Some common indicators of stress include aggression, defensive postures like hissing or puffing up, reduced appetite, restlessness, attempts to hide in dark corners, color changes, rapid or open-mouth breathing, and other observable behavioral changes.

To minimize stress during handling, a thoughtful and gradual approach is essential. Reptiles should be acclimated to handling gradually, starting with short sessions and slowly increasing the duration as they become more accustomed to the experience. Avoiding sudden movements and loud noises is crucial, as these can startle or agitate the reptile. Maintaining a respectful distance until the animal is calm and ready for handling helps foster a sense of security.

Choosing the optimal timing for handling is another key consideration. Reptiles are most relaxed during certain periods, such as after basking or when they are less active. Handling during these times minimizes the likelihood of encountering a stressed or agitated reptile.

Proper support for the reptile's body during handling is paramount to prevent discomfort or injury. Using both hands to provide balanced support ensures that the reptile feels secure and at ease. Handling should always take place in a secure and controlled environment, such as a designated handling area or a safe enclosure.

Limiting the frequency of handling is essential to prevent chronic stress. Reptiles need ample time to rest and recover between handling sessions. Paying close attention to the reptile's body language and behavior during handling is vital. If signs of stress are clear, it's best to gently return the reptile to its enclosure to prevent further distress.

Positive reinforcement techniques can be incredibly effective in creating positive associations with handling. Offering favorite treats or rewards can help the reptile feel more at ease during the process. It's important to recognize that each reptile is unique and may have varying levels of tolerance for handling. Tailoring the approach to the individual's preferences and comfort is key to a successful and low-stress experience.

In cases where handling proves challenging or concerns arise, seeking guidance from experienced reptile handlers or herpetologists is a prudent course of action. Their expertise can offer valuable insights and solutions to ensure the welfare and happiness of reptiles while fostering a positive and safe handling experience.

Tips for Taming Shy or Aggressive Reptiles

Strategies for building trust with timid reptiles

Reptiles are fascinating creatures that have been around for millions of years. These cold-blooded animals come in all shapes and sizes, from tiny geckos to massive crocodiles. However, many reptiles are naturally timid and cautious, making it a challenge to build trust with them. In this guide, we will explore strategies for building trust with these shy reptiles.

Before diving into specific strategies, it's crucial to understand why some reptiles are timid in the first place. Timidity in reptiles often stems from their natural instincts for self-preservation. In the wild, reptiles are vulnerable to predators, so they tend to be cautious and avoid unnecessary risks. This innate behavior can make it difficult for them to trust humans, as they see us as potential threats.

When working with timid reptiles, patience is your most valuable asset. Building trust takes time, and you must be willing to invest in it. Rushing the process can lead to stress and fear in the reptile, making it even more challenging to gain their trust. Take things slow and allow the reptile to acclimate to your presence at its own pace.

One of the first steps in building trust with a timid reptile is to respect their personal space. Avoid sudden movements or loud noises that can startle them. Give them room to retreat if they feel uncomfortable. Over time, as they become more accustomed to your presence, they may begin to venture closer to you on their own.

When interacting with timid reptiles, use non-threatening gestures to signal your intentions. Slowly extend your hand towards them, palm down, and allow them to approach you if they feel comfortable. Avoid making sudden, jerky movements or trying to grab them, as this will only increase their fear.

Food can be a powerful tool in building trust with timid reptiles. Find out what their favorite treats are and offer them by hand. This can help the reptile associate your presence with positive experiences. Gradually, they may become more comfortable approaching you in anticipation of food.

Establishing a consistent routine can also help build trust. Reptiles thrive on predictability, so try to handle and feed them at the same times each day. This routine will create a sense of security for the reptile, as they will know what to expect from you.

It's essential to recognize that not all timid reptiles will become completely comfortable with close human interaction. Some may always prefer to maintain a certain distance. It's crucial to respect their boundaries and not push them beyond their comfort zone. Building trust doesn't necessarily mean turning a shy reptile into a cuddly companion; it means creating a positive and safe environment for them.

Reinforce positive behavior with praise and rewards. When the reptile shows signs of trust, such as approaching you without hesitation, offer verbal praise and a treat. This positive reinforcement will encourage them to continue building trust with you.

Never use punishment or negative reinforcement with timid reptiles. It will only cause fear and erode any trust you've built. Instead, focus on creating a safe and nurturing environment that encourages trust through positive interactions.

Spend time observing the reptile in their natural habitat, whether it's a terrarium or an outdoor enclosure. This will help you better understand their behavior and preferences. The more you know about your reptile, the easier it will be to anticipate their needs and build trust.

If you're struggling to build trust with a particularly timid reptile, don't hesitate to seek professional guidance. Experienced herpetologists or reptile experts can provide valuable advice and insights according to your specific situation.

Building trust with timid reptiles is a rewarding endeavor that requires patience, respect, and understanding. By taking the time to understand their instincts and preferences, respecting their boundaries, and using positive reinforcement, you can establish a strong bond with these fascinating creatures. Remember that trust is a two-way street, and with time and dedication, you can create a trusting and enriching relationship with your shy reptile companion.

Addressing aggressive behavior through positive reinforcement

Aggression in reptiles is a behavior that can be challenging to deal with, and it's important to approach it with care and understanding. Unlike mammals or birds, reptiles may display aggression in ways that are not immediately obvious to us. This aggression can stem from various factors, including fear, stress, discomfort, or territorial instincts. To provide the best care for your reptile, it's essential to recognize and address these aggressive behaviors.

Positive reinforcement is a valuable technique in reptile care that can help mitigate aggressive behavior. This method involves rewarding desirable behaviors to encourage their repetition while discouraging or redirecting undesirable behaviors. It can be particularly effective in promoting better behavior and reducing aggression in reptiles.

To successfully implement positive reinforcement in reptile care, consistency is crucial. Reptiles, like all animals, thrive on routine and predictability. When using positive reinforcement, it's important to provide rewards consistently for the desired behaviors and avoid rewarding or reacting to aggressive actions. Patience is equally important because reptiles may take time to change their behavior, and rushing the process can be counterproductive.

The application of positive reinforcement in reptile care should be tailored to the specific species and individual reptile's needs and preferences. For instance, if you have a territorial reptile, such as a turtle or iguana, that displays aggression when you approach its enclosure, positive reinforcement may involve offering treats or gentle praise when the reptile remains calm during your visits. Over time, the reptile may associate your presence with positive experiences and become less aggressive.

It's essential to consider the unique characteristics of each reptile species. Some reptiles may be more sensitive and require a softer touch, while others may respond well to gentle handling and food rewards.

Understanding the temperament and behavior of your specific reptile is crucial for applying positive reinforcement effectively.

While positive reinforcement can be a valuable tool in addressing aggression in reptiles, it's important to acknowledge that not all cases can be resolved through this method alone. Some reptiles may have underlying health issues or severe behavioral problems that require professional intervention. In such cases, consulting with a reptile veterinarian or a herpetologist is essential to ensure the wellbeing of the reptile.

Addressing aggressive behavior in reptiles is an integral aspect of ultimate reptile care. Aggression in reptiles can have various underlying causes, including fear, stress, discomfort, or territorial instincts. Positive reinforcement, when used correctly and consistently, can be a valuable tool for promoting better behavior in reptiles. By rewarding calm and non-aggressive behaviors and creating a stress-free environment, reptile owners and enthusiasts can help their reptiles feel more secure and reduce aggressive tendencies. However, it's crucial to remember that each reptile is unique, and professional guidance should be sought in cases of severe aggression or persistent issues to provide the best possible care for these remarkable creatures.

Gradual desensitization techniques for nervous reptiles

Reptiles, with their diverse and fascinating array of species, have become increasingly popular as pets. Their unique characteristics and captivating behaviors draw many reptile enthusiasts into the world of herpetology. However, one common challenge that reptile owners may encounter is dealing with nervous behavior in their scaly companions.

Nervousness in reptiles can manifest in various ways, depending on the species and individual temperament. It often includes behaviors such as hiding, hissing, puffing up, or even striking or biting when they feel threatened or stressed. These reactions can be disheartening for reptile owners who want to provide the best possible care for their pets. Fortunately, gradual desensitization techniques can be valuable tools in helping nervous reptiles become more comfortable in their environment and with human interaction.

Before diving into the techniques of gradual desensitization, it's essential to grasp the underlying causes of nervous behavior in reptiles. Unlike mammals or birds, reptiles are ectothermic, meaning they rely on external sources of heat to regulate their body temperature. This dependence on environmental conditions, such as temperature and humidity, makes them particularly sensitive to changes in their surroundings.

Reptiles are also creatures with millions of years of evolutionary history, and most have evolved to be cautious animals. In the wild, reptiles often fall prey to predators, and this has instilled in them an innate instinct for self-preservation. This instinct can lead to nervous behavior when they perceive potential threats, including humans.

Recognizing these natural instincts is crucial when working with nervous reptiles. It helps reptile owners understand that nervous behavior is not a reflection of a reptile's dislike or aggression toward them but rather a survival mechanism deeply ingrained in their biology.

A fundamental step in desensitizing nervous reptiles is ensuring they have an optimal environment. Reptiles require an environment that closely mimics their natural habitat to thrive. This includes maintaining appropriate temperature and humidity levels, as well as offering hiding spots and suitable substrates.

When reptiles are kept in environments that do not meet their specific needs, they can become stressed, which can make nervous behavior worse. For example, a reptile may feel threatened if it cannot adequately thermoregulate due to incorrect temperatures in its enclosure. Providing an optimal environment is a key component of alleviating stress and, consequently, nervousness in reptiles.

Creating a suitable environment also involves offering appropriate hiding spots. These hiding spots serve as safe havens for reptiles when they feel overwhelmed or vulnerable. Having a secure place to retreat to can reduce their overall stress levels and make them feel more secure.

Desensitization begins with a slow and gradual introduction to human presence. It's essential to start slowly and respect the reptile's boundaries. During the initial stages, this may involve simply sitting near the reptile's enclosure without any direct interaction. The goal is to let the reptile become accustomed to your presence without feeling threatened.

For particularly timid reptiles, it can be beneficial to use a barrier between you and the reptile. A clear acrylic sheet or glass can serve as a visual barrier, allowing the reptile to observe you without direct contact. Over time, the reptile will become more familiar with your presence, and its anxiety may gradually decrease.

Minimizing handling is crucial during the early stages of desensitization, especially for reptiles that exhibit nervous behavior. Many reptiles find handling highly stressful, and it can further exacerbate their anxiety. As such, it's advisable to refrain from excessive handling until the reptile has become more comfortable with your presence.

When handling does occur, it should be gentle and brief. Allowing the reptile to explore and move at its own pace is essential. During these early interactions, it's crucial to pay close attention to the reptile's body language. Signs of distress or discomfort, such as rapid breathing, defensive postures, or color changes, should be taken seriously. If the reptile displays these signs, it's best to return it to its enclosure and try again at a later time.

Positive reinforcement is a powerful tool in the desensitization process for nervous reptiles. This technique involves rewarding calm and non-aggressive behavior with treats or gentle verbal praise. The goal is to create a positive association with human interaction, helping the reptile feel more at ease when you are around.

For instance, if you have a nervous gecko, you can offer a small treat when it ventures out of its hiding spot while you are nearby. Over time, the gecko may begin to associate your presence with positive experiences and rewards.

As the reptile becomes more comfortable with your presence and handling, you can gradually increase the level of interaction. This may involve gentle touches or allowing the reptile to crawl onto your hand. However, it's essential to remain attuned to the reptile's body language during these interactions. If it displays signs of distress or discomfort, it's crucial to respond by minimizing the interaction and providing a safe retreat.

Desensitization techniques require a great deal of patience and observation. Each reptile is unique, and the time it takes to reduce nervous behavior will vary. Being attentive to the reptile's cues, such as changes in posture, coloration, or vocalizations, can help you gauge its comfort level and adjust your approach accordingly.

It's essential to remember that desensitization is not a one-size-fits-all process. Some reptiles may progress more quickly, while others may require more time and patience. The key is to remain patient, consistent, and gentle throughout the process.

In some cases, despite your best efforts, nervous behavior in reptiles may persist or even worsen. In such instances, it is advisable to seek consultation with reptile experts, such as herpetologists or veterinarians with reptile expertise. These professionals can provide guidance, advice, and potential solutions tailored to your specific reptile's needs.

Expert consultation is particularly crucial if you suspect that there may be underlying health issues contributing to the reptile's nervous behavior. Addressing these issues is essential for the overall well-being of the reptile.

Bonding with Your Pet

Understanding reptile communication and body language

Reptiles, with their ancient lineage and diverse species, have evolved unique ways of communicating with each other and their environment. While reptile communication may not be as readily apparent or expressive as that of mammals or birds, it is a fascinating and essential aspect of their behavior. By delving into the intricacies of reptile communication and body language, we can gain insight into the needs, emotions, and social interactions of these remarkable creatures.

Reptiles are well-known for their diverse range of colors and patterns, which often serve as visual signals to convey information. Changes in coloration can be particularly striking and meaningful in reptiles. For example, chameleons are famous for their ability to change color based on their mood, temperature, and social interactions.

In many reptiles, coloration changes can signify stress, aggression, or readiness to mate. For instance, during mating displays, male anole lizards may exhibit vibrant colors to attract females. In contrast, darker colors or patterns may indicate aggression or territorial behavior in various species.

Body posture is another crucial element of visual communication in reptiles. Defensive postures, such as puffing up or arching the back, are often used to deter potential predators or competitors. Conversely, relaxed body postures, with limbs extended and a calm demeanor, indicate a reptile's comfort and contentment.

While not as prominent as visual cues, chemical signals play a significant role in reptile communication. Reptiles, like snakes and lizards, can produce and detect pheromones—chemical substances that convey information about their reproductive status, territorial boundaries, and readiness to mate.

In reptiles, pheromones are often secreted through specialized glands located in various parts of the body, such as the cloaca. Male and female reptiles can release pheromones to signal their receptivity to mating, helping potential mates locate each other in their environment. Additionally, territorial reptiles may use pheromones to mark their territory boundaries, warning others to stay away.

While reptiles are not typically known for vocalizations like birds or mammals, some species do produce sounds to communicate. These vocalizations can serve various purposes, from mating calls to territorial disputes.

For example, frogs and toads, which are classified as amphibians rather than reptiles but share some similarities, are known for their distinctive croaking calls during the breeding season. In reptiles, some species of geckos and anoles may produce chirping or clicking sounds as part of their courtship rituals. In these cases, vocalizations are used to attract potential mates and establish dominance.

Snakes, on the other hand, are generally not vocal in the traditional sense. However, they can rattle when threatened or provoked, serving as a warning to potential predators or competitors. While not a melodic communication method, hissing is an effective means of deterring threats.

Tactile communication plays a crucial role in reptile interactions, particularly between individuals within the same species. Reptiles may use physical touch and gestures to convey information about dominance, submission, or mating readiness.

Courtship rituals in reptiles often involve tactile communication. For example, male turtles may stroke the faces or necks of females with their long claws during the mating process. In some species of snakes, males engage in ritualistic combat where they use their bodies to push and wrestle with each other, determining which individual will have the opportunity to mate with a female. Similarly, in certain lizard species, males may exhibit territorial or courtship behaviors that involve nipping at the female's neck or engaging in physical displays to establish dominance and secure mating rights. These behaviors are essential aspects of their reproductive strategies and serve to regulate breeding opportunities within their populations.

Intraspecies dominance hierarchies may be established through physical gestures, such as head-bobbing in lizards or the use of body size and posture in crocodilians. These gestures are essential for maintaining social order within a group or population.

Social interactions among reptiles often involve complex displays of body language and behavior. These displays are crucial for establishing dominance, courtship, and territorial boundaries. Agonistic displays, which are often ritualized behaviors, serve to prevent physical confrontations and minimize the risk of injury.

An example of agonistic behavior can be observed in male iguanas, which often engage in elaborate displays of head-bobbing, dewlap extensions, and body inflation to establish dominance. The winner of these displays gains access to preferred basking sites and mating opportunities without resorting to physical combat.

Similarly, male anole lizards engage in push-up displays to signal their presence and establish territories. These displays communicate to other males in the vicinity that the territory is already claimed, reducing the likelihood of direct confrontations.

Understanding reptile communication and body language is not only valuable for those observing these animals in the wild but also for reptile owners in a captive setting. Recognizing signs of stress, discomfort, or illness in pet reptiles is essential for their wellbeing.

For example, if a captive snake is repeatedly hissing and striking at its enclosure, it may be signalling distress or a feeling of vulnerability. Changes in coloration or posture can also indicate that a reptile is experiencing stress due to inadequate environmental conditions.

In captivity, reptile owners can provide a more enriching environment by replicating natural behaviors and social interactions as closely as possible. For example, providing hiding spots, basking areas, and appropriate substrates can help reptiles feel more secure and reduce stress.

Additionally, understanding the reproductive behaviors and seasonal cues of pet reptiles can be important for those interested in breeding them. Properly timed temperature and lighting adjustments can simulate natural breeding seasons, encouraging courtship and mating behavior.

Building a strong bond through positive interactions

Reptiles, with their unique characteristics and captivating behaviors, have become increasingly popular as pets. However, their cold-blooded reputation sometimes leads to misconceptions about their capacity for forming bonds with their human caregivers. While reptiles may not express affection in the same way as pets such as dogs, they are capable of forming strong bonds with those who care for them. Building a strong bond with a reptile involves understanding their needs, providing a nurturing environment, and engaging in positive interactions that promote trust and wellbeing.

Before embarking on the journey of building a strong bond with a reptile, it's essential to understand their specific needs and preferences. Reptiles are ectothermic, meaning they rely on external sources of heat to regulate their body temperature. Maintaining the correct temperature gradient within their enclosure is crucial for their health and wellbeing.

Each species of reptile has its own temperature and humidity requirements, which should be researched and carefully met. Providing an optimal environment ensures that your reptile is comfortable and stress-free, laying the foundation for a positive bond.

A nurturing environment goes beyond temperature control. Reptiles require appropriate substrates, hiding spots, and access to clean water to thrive. These elements contribute to their sense of security and wellbeing, which, in turn, impacts their ability to form a bond with their caregivers.

Hiding spots, such as caves or burrows, provide reptiles with a retreat where they can feel safe and secure. Offering various hiding spots within their enclosure allows them to choose their preferred resting place, promoting a sense of control over their environment.

Additionally, providing appropriate substrates for burrowing or basking can mimic their natural habitat, making them feel more at home. Reptiles that feel comfortable in their environment are more likely to engage in positive interactions with their caregivers.

Building a strong bond with a reptile is a gradual process that requires patience, consistency, and positive interactions. While reptiles may not exhibit affection in the same way mammals do, they can still form a deep connection with their caregivers.

One of the most crucial aspects of positive interactions is respecting the reptile's boundaries. Each reptile has its own temperament and comfort level with human contact. Observing their body language and cues is essential in determining when they are receptive to interaction and when they need space.

Positive interactions can involve gentle handling, feeding, and even environmental enrichment. For example, offering live insects to a reptile that enjoys hunting can provide mental stimulation and promote bonding through the act of providing food.

To build a strong bond with a reptile, it's crucial to understand their body language and communication cues. While reptiles may not have facial expressions or vocalizations like mammals, they convey information through their posture, coloration, and behavior.

For example, a reptile that is relaxed and content will display open body posture, with limbs extended and a calm demeanor. On the other hand, a stressed or threatened reptile may exhibit defensive behaviors, such as hissing, puffing up, or displaying aggressive postures.

Understanding these cues allows caregivers to gauge the reptile's comfort level during interactions. It's important to recognize signs of stress and respond by giving the reptile space and time to calm down. This not only prevents potential harm but also promotes trust and a positive bond.

Consistency and routine are essential components of building a strong bond with a reptile. Reptiles thrive on predictability and routine, and they can become stressed if their environment or interactions are constantly changing.

Establishing a regular feeding schedule, maintaining consistent lighting and temperature cycles, and providing a stable environment all contribute to a reptile's sense of security. When a reptile can predict when and how its needs will be met, it is more likely to form a bond of trust with its caregiver.

Reptiles, like all animals, are individuals with their own personalities and preferences. Building a bond involves recognizing and respecting these unique characteristics.

Some reptiles may be naturally more outgoing and curious, while others are more reserved. Some may enjoy being handled and seek out interaction, while others may prefer to observe from a distance. It's essential to adapt your approach based on the individual needs and comfort level of your reptile.

For example, a friendly and sociable reptile may thrive on gentle handling and may even seek out human contact. In contrast, a shy and introverted reptile may require a quieter and more patient approach, allowing it to gradually become accustomed to human presence and interaction.

Positive reinforcement is a powerful tool in building a strong bond with a reptile. This technique involves rewarding desirable behaviors to encourage their repetition. While reptiles may not understand praise or affection in the same way dogs do, they can still associate positive experiences with specific actions.

For instance, when a reptile willingly climbs onto your

hand or comes out of its hiding spot to explore when you're nearby, offering a small treat as a reward can create a positive association with human interaction. Over time, the reptile may come to anticipate positive experiences during these interactions, strengthening the bond between you and your pet.

Recognizing signs of affection and trust

Reptiles, with their ancient and diverse lineage, are often perceived as creatures that lack the capacity for affection or trust. However, this common misconception overlooks the subtle yet meaningful ways in which reptiles express these emotions. While reptiles may not display affection in the same overt manner as dogs or other mammals, they can and do form bonds with their caregivers. Recognizing the signs of affection and trust in reptiles requires a deeper understanding of their behaviors, body language, and unique expressions of emotion.

To recognize signs of affection and trust in reptiles, it's crucial to first understand their natural behaviors and instincts. Reptiles are ectothermic, meaning they rely on external sources of heat to regulate their body temperature. This dependence on environmental conditions has shaped their behaviors and daily routines.

Reptiles are also creatures with millions of years of evolutionary history, and many have evolved to be cautious animals. In the wild, reptiles often fall prey to predators, which has instilled in them an innate instinct for self-preservation. Recognizing these instincts is essential when assessing their expressions of emotion.

One of the primary signs of affection and trust in reptiles is the consistency in their behavior around their caregivers. Reptiles are creatures of habit and thrive on predictability. When they become accustomed to the presence and routines of their caregivers, it's a strong indicator that they trust and feel comfortable around them.

For example, if a pet reptile approaches its caregiver without displaying signs of stress or defensive behaviors, it suggests that the reptile has established a level of trust. Reptiles often seek consistency and routine, and when they associate their caregivers with positive experiences, their behavior reflects this sense of trust.

Reptiles can communicate their emotional state through body language. When a reptile feels comfortable and at ease, it typically exhibits relaxed body language. This may include extending its limbs, having a calm demeanor, and displaying open postures.

For example, a reptile that lounges with its limbs extended and doesn't show defensive postures, such as puffing up or hissing, is more likely to be comfortable in its caregiver's presence. This relaxed body language is a clear sign that the reptile trusts and feels at ease with its human companion.

Appetite and feeding behavior can also reveal a lot about a reptile's level of trust and comfort with its caregiver. When a reptile readily accepts food from its caregiver's hand, it signifies a significant level of trust. This behavior demonstrates that the reptile associates the caregiver with positive experiences, such as mealtime.

Furthermore, a reptile that eagerly approaches its caregiver during feeding time or waits expectantly for food demonstrates both trust and a bond. The reptile recognizes the caregiver as a source of nourishment and security, solidifying the bond between them.

Reptiles that actively engage in exploration and interaction with their caregivers are often demonstrating affection and trust. When a reptile willingly climbs onto a caregiver's hand or explores its environment without fear or hesitation, it reflects a level of comfort and confidence in the caregiver's presence.

For example, a pet lizard that eagerly ventures out of its enclosure to explore when its caregiver is nearby is demonstrating a sense of trust and attachment. The reptile seeks out interaction and is willing to explore the world beyond its habitat with the caregiver as a companion.

Tolerance of handling is a significant indicator of trust in reptiles. While not all reptiles are naturally inclined to enjoy being handled, those that allow handling without exhibiting stress or defensive behaviors are likely demonstrating a bond of trust.

Reptiles that willingly sit on their caregiver's hand, shoulder, or lap without struggling or trying to escape are displaying a high level of trust. Tolerating handling indicates that the reptile views the caregiver as a source of comfort and security, rather than a threat.

While reptiles are not typically known for vocalizations like birds or mammals, some species do produce sounds as a means of communication. Understanding these vocalizations can provide insight into a reptile's emotional state.

For example, certain geckos and anoles are known to produce chirping or clicking sounds during courtship rituals or interactions with their caregivers. While not all reptiles vocalize, those that do may use these sounds to express their emotions, including a sense of trust and attachment.

It's important to recognize that each reptile is unique, with its own personality and preferences. While some reptiles may readily demonstrate signs of affection and trust, others may be more reserved or take longer to establish a bond.

Respecting the individuality of each reptile is crucial in building trust and fostering affection. It's essential to adapt your approach based on the reptile's temperament and comfort level with human contact. Some reptiles may require more time and patience to develop a strong bond, while others may be naturally more outgoing.

Building a bond of affection and trust with a reptile is a gradual process that requires time and consistency. Consistent care routines, positive interactions, and a nurturing environment all contribute to the development of a strong bond.

Reptiles may take time to become accustomed to their caregivers and feel secure in their presence. Patience is key, as the strength of the bond often deepens over time. As the reptile becomes more familiar with the caregiver and associates them with positive experiences, signs of trust and affection become more apparent.

Chapter 5

Healthcare and Common Health Issues

Healthcare for reptiles involves providing proper nutrition, maintaining optimal environmental conditions, and seeking veterinary care when necessary. Common health issues in reptiles include metabolic bone disease, respiratory infections, parasites, and skin problems. Regular check-ups and attentive care can help prevent and address these issues, ensuring the well-being of your reptilian companion.

Regular Check-ups and Veterinary Care

The frequency of veterinary visits for different reptile species

Reptile ownership comes with the responsibility of ensuring the well-being of these unique creatures. Part of that responsibility involves regular veterinary care to monitor their health, address potential issues, and provide preventative measures. However, the frequency of veterinary visits can vary significantly among different reptile species, depending on their individual needs, lifespan, and susceptibility to health problems. Understanding when and how often to take your reptile to the veterinarian is essential for providing proper care.

Reptiles encompass a wide range of species, each with its own specific needs and health considerations. Consequently, the frequency of veterinary visits can differ significantly based on the type of reptile you own.

For example, species like turtles and tortoises tend to be long-lived, with some individuals living for several decades or even over a century. These reptiles are vulnerable when they are juveniles and might need more check-ups, but during their adult lives often require fewer visits to the vet. However, regular monitoring of their health becomes increasingly important as they age, as they may develop age-related conditions.

In contrast, certain snake species, such as ball pythons or boas, may have lifespans ranging from 20 to 30 years or more. Regular veterinary visits, particularly during their juvenile and adult stages, are crucial to address issues like parasites, respiratory infections, and reproductive health.

Lizards, such as bearded dragons or iguanas, fall into various size categories, with some being relatively small and others growing quite large. The frequency of veterinary visits may depend on the size and species of the lizard, as well as their susceptibility to specific health problems.

It's essential to research and understand the specific needs and potential health concerns of your reptile species to determine an appropriate veterinary care schedule. For optimal reptile healthcare, it can be advantageous to find a veterinarian who specializes in reptiles or exotics, as they possess specialized knowledge and experience that can ensure your reptile receives the best possible care and treatment.

The life stage of your reptile also influences the frequency of veterinary visits. Juvenile reptiles, like human infants, often require more frequent check-ups than their adult counterparts. This is because they are more susceptible to various health issues during their growth and development.

For example, young reptiles may need frequent assessments to monitor their growth, ensure they are shedding properly, and address any nutritional deficiencies. They may also require periodic parasite screenings, as these can be more common in juveniles.

As reptiles reach adulthood, their veterinary needs may

become less frequent, depending on their species and individual health. However, regular wellness exams are still essential to catch potential issues early and ensure their long-term health and well-being.

For reptile species that reproduce including snakes, lizards, and turtles, reproductive health considerations can impact the frequency of veterinary visits. Breeding reptiles require specialized care and may need more frequent veterinary assessments during the breeding season.

Female reptiles, in particular, may require additional veterinary attention to monitor their reproductive health and ensure successful breeding. Egg-laying species, like many turtles and lizards, can experience complications during egg laying, such as egg binding. Timely veterinary intervention is critical in such cases.

Breeding reptiles should also be screened for potential infections or diseases that can affect their reproductive success and the health of their offspring. This additional care and monitoring during the breeding season may necessitate more frequent veterinary visits.

The specific health concerns and common issues associated with different reptile species can also influence the frequency of veterinary visits. Some health problems are more prevalent in certain types of reptiles, and regular veterinary check-ups can help prevent or address these issues.

For example, Metabolic Bone Disease (MBD) is a common concern in reptiles like iguanas and bearded dragons. Regular veterinary visits can include assessments of calcium levels, bone health, and UVB lighting to prevent and manage

MBD.

Respiratory infections, another common health issue in reptiles, may require more frequent veterinary attention for species like snakes and turtles. These infections can be challenging to detect in their early stages, making regular check-ups essential for prompt treatment.

Parasites, such as mites or internal worms, can affect various reptile species. Routine parasite screenings, especially for outdoor or wild-caught reptiles, are crucial to prevent infestations and related health problems.

Preventative care is a significant factor in determining the frequency of veterinary visits for reptiles. Routine check-ups provide an opportunity for veterinarians to assess overall health, identify potential concerns, and offer guidance on proper husbandry practices.

Annual or biannual visits may be suitable for many reptile species to receive preventative care, including physical exams, blood tests, and fecal examinations. These visits allow for early detection of health issues and the implementation of preventive measures, such as vaccinations or adjustments to diet and habitat.

Reptile owners can also benefit from these visits by receiving education and guidance on proper nutrition, habitat setup, and hygiene practices. Preventative care is essential for maintaining the health and longevity of pet reptiles.

In addition to routine veterinary visits, reptile owners should be prepared for emergency situations. Reptiles can be prone to sudden health crises, such as trauma, infections, or egg-related complications, that require immediate medical attention.

Having a trusted reptile veterinarian and understanding their emergency contact information is essential for prompt response in critical situations. Familiarity with potential signs of distress or illness in your reptile can also help you recognize when immediate veterinary care is necessary.

Routine health checklists for at-home monitoring

Maintaining the health and well-being of your pet reptile requires regular monitoring and attentive care. While professional veterinary visits are essential, at-home monitoring plays a vital role in ensuring your reptile's continued health between check-ups. Establishing a routine health checklist for at home monitoring helps you observe changes in behavior, appearance, and environment, allowing you to identify potential issues early and provide timely care. In this comprehensive guide, we will explore the key aspects of a routine health checklist for reptiles.

Temperature and humidity levels are critical for reptiles, as they are ectothermic and rely on external conditions to regulate their body temperature. Different reptile species have specific temperature and humidity requirements that mimic their natural habitats. It is crucial to monitor and maintain these conditions within the appropriate range.

Regularly check the temperature gradient within your reptile's enclosure. Ensure that there are warm basking spots and cooler areas to allow your reptile to thermoregulate. A digital thermometer with probes can provide accurate temperature readings in different areas of the enclosure.

Humidity levels are equally important, as they can impact your reptile's hydration and skin health. Use a hygrometer to measure humidity, and be aware of the specific requirements for your reptile species. Some reptiles, like chameleons, require higher humidity levels than others.

Monitoring your reptile's body weight and growth is an essential part of at-home health checks. Regular weighing can help detect changes in your reptile's condition, including weight loss or gain, which may indicate health issues.

Use a digital kitchen scale to weigh your reptile periodically. Keep a record of their weight to track any significant changes over time. Growth patterns can also provide insights into your reptile's overall health and development, especially in young reptiles.

Observing your reptile's feeding habits and dietary preferences is crucial for monitoring their health. Reptiles may exhibit changes in appetite, food refusal, or alterations in dietary choices when they are unwell.

Keep a feeding log to record the type and amount of food your reptile consumes. Note any instances of food refusal or changes in eating patterns. Uneaten food can be a sign of stress, illness, or potential digestive problems.

Additionally, ensure that you provide a balanced and species-appropriate diet for your reptile. Consult with a reptile veterinarian or a reputable source to determine the best nutritional plan for your specific species.

Many reptiles shed their skin periodically as they grow. Monitoring the shedding process and the condition of your reptile's skin is essential. Proper shedding indicates good health, while difficulties in shedding can be a sign of dehydration or skin issues.

Regularly inspect your reptile's skin for any retained shed, especially around the eyes, toes, and tail tip. Retained shed can constrict circulation and lead to serious problems. Ensure that your reptile has access to a suitable shedding substrate, such as damp moss or a shedding box.

Additionally, look for any signs of skin abnormalities, such as lesions, blisters, or discoloration. These can be indicators of underlying health concerns or skin infections.

Reptile behavior can provide valuable insights into their overall health and wellbeing. Establishing a baseline for your reptile's typical behavior allows you to detect any deviations from their normal patterns.

Observe your reptile's activity level, basking behavior, and interactions with their environment. Changes in behavior, such as increased lethargy, reduced appetite, excessive hiding, or aggression, can signal health issues.

Keep an eye out for any abnormal postures or movements, such as difficulty climbing, uncoordinated limb use, or tremors. These can be indications of musculoskeletal or neurological problems.

Respiratory health is a critical aspect of reptile care. Respiratory infections are relatively common in some reptile species and can be life-threatening if left untreated.

Regularly monitor your reptile's breathing rate and pattern. Healthy reptiles should exhibit regular, quiet breathing without any audible wheezing, coughing, or labored breathing. If you notice any signs of respiratory distress, consult a veterinarian promptly.

Examining your reptile's excrement and urination is another essential part of at-home monitoring. Changes in fecal or urinary patterns can be indicative of digestive issues, parasitic infections, or metabolic problems.

Observe the color, consistency, and frequency of your reptile's excrement. Any signs of diarrhea, blood in feces, or drastic changes in excrement should be noted.

Monitor urination patterns and note any changes in the color or frequency of urates (white, chalky material) and urine.

Dehydration can lead to concentrated urates, while excessive urination may indicate kidney issues.

Reptiles rely on their enclosure's environmental conditions to thrive. Regularly check and maintain the habitat to ensure that it meets your reptile's needs.

Inspect heating elements, such as heat lamps or heat mats, to ensure they are functioning correctly and providing the appropriate temperature gradient.

Check that UVB bulbs are within their recommended lifespan, as expired bulbs may not provide adequate UVB radiation, which is essential for calcium metabolism.

Keep the enclosure clean and hygienic, removing

waste and any uneaten food promptly. Maintaining proper hygiene helps prevent bacterial and fungal infections.

If you house multiple reptiles together, monitor their social interactions. Aggression, bullying, or injuries can occur in multi-reptile enclosures.

Observe how your reptiles interact with each other, especially during feeding and basking times. Pay attention to any signs of aggression, such as biting, tail lashing, or territorial disputes.

In case of injuries or signs of stress, consider providing separate enclosures or consulting with a reptile veterinarian for guidance on managing social dynamics.

The Importance of Finding a Reptile Experienced Veterinarian

Caring for a pet reptile is a unique and rewarding experience, but it also comes with the responsibility of ensuring their health and well-being. One of the most crucial aspects of reptile ownership is finding a veterinarian with expertise in treating these cold-blooded creatures. Reptiles have specific health requirements and are prone to unique ailments, making it essential to seek the care of a reptile experienced veterinarian. In this article, we will explore the importance of finding such a specialized veterinarian and the benefits it brings to both you and your scaly companion.

Reptiles are a diverse group of animals, and the care they require can vary significantly from that of more traditional pets like cats or dogs. A reptile-experienced veterinarian possesses specialized knowledge and expertise in the anatomy, physiology, and behavior of reptiles. This expertise is vital for accurate diagnoses, effective treatment plans, and preventive care measures.

Unlike mammals, reptiles often mask signs of illness or discomfort, making it challenging to detect health issues. Reptile experienced veterinarians have the knowledge and experience to recognize subtle signs of illness and perform thorough examinations to uncover underlying problems. Their familiarity with reptile-specific diseases and health conditions ensures a more accurate assessment of your pet's health.

Reptile-experienced veterinarians typically have access to specialized diagnostic equipment and tools specifically designed for reptile care. This includes equipment for radiography (X-rays), ultrasonography, endoscopy, and blood tests tailored to the unique requirements of reptiles. Having access to these tools allows for more accurate and comprehensive assessments of your reptile's health.

For example, radiography can help identify bone abnormalities or the presence of egg-related issues in reptiles. Ultrasonography is essential for evaluating reproductive health in female reptiles and diagnosing egg binding or ovarian issues. These diagnostic capabilities are critical for timely intervention and treatment.

Reptile-experienced veterinarians also have a deep understanding of the specific husbandry needs of various reptile species. They can provide guidance on habitat setup, lighting, temperature gradients, humidity levels, and dietary requirements that are tailored to your pet's species and individual needs.

Correct husbandry is essential for preventing health issues in reptiles. A veterinarian experienced in reptile care can offer valuable advice on creating an environment that promotes your reptile's wellbeing, reducing the risk of stress-related problems and metabolic disorders.

Just like with other pets, preventive care is crucial for maintaining your reptile's health and preventing potential problems. Reptile experienced veterinarians can establish a wellness plan for your pet, including regular check-ups, vaccinations (if applicable), and parasite screenings.

Regular wellness exams allow the veterinarian to monitor your reptile's growth, weight, and overall condition over time. Early detection of health issues can lead to more effective treatment and better outcomes. Preventive care also includes discussions about nutrition, supplementation, and environmental enrichment to optimize your reptile's quality of life.

Reptiles can experience emergencies and sudden health crises, just like any other pet. Having a reptile-experienced veterinarian means you can access prompt and appropriate care in emergencies. They are equipped to handle issues such as trauma, respiratory distress, egg-related complications, and metabolic imbalances.

Timely interventions can be life-saving for reptiles, as some conditions can progress rapidly. An experienced reptile veterinarian is prepared to provide critical care and emergency procedures to stabilize your pet's condition and initiate treatment.

Reptile-experienced veterinarians are often passionate about reptiles and have a deep understanding of the unique bond that exists between reptile owners and their pets. They approach reptile care with compassion and empathy, recognizing the importance of these creatures in people's lives.

Reptile owners may have specific concerns or questions related to their pets, and an experienced veterinarian can provide reassurance and guidance. They understand the nuances of reptile behavior and can help interpret subtle signs of distress or illness, providing peace of mind to owners.

Signs of a Healthy Reptile

Detailed guide to recognizing physical and behavioral indicators of health

Caring for a pet reptile is a unique and rewarding experience that comes with a distinctive set of responsibilities. Beyond providing the right habitat and proper diet, reptile owners must be vigilant in monitoring their pet's physical and behavioral well-being.

Unlike mammals, reptiles often conceal signs of illness, making it crucial for owners to be adept at recognizing subtle indicators that something may be amiss. In this comprehensive guide, we will delve into the physical and behavioral cues that can help you assess the health of your reptilian companion.

Physical indicators play a vital role in assessing the overall health of your reptile. Regularly monitoring your pet's body weight and condition is a fundamental aspect of this assessment. Weight loss or gain can be early signs of health issues, and maintaining a healthy body weight is essential for your reptile's well-being. A well-proportioned body with no visible ribs or bones protruding is a sign of a healthy reptile.

The skin and scales of your reptile provide valuable information about their health. Observe any changes in skin color, texture, or pigmentation. A healthy reptile should have smooth, vibrant, and well-hydrated skin. Dry, flaky, or discolored skin may indicate dehydration or underlying health problems. Proper shedding, a regular process for most reptiles, is another indicator of good health. Ensure that your reptile is shedding complete and intact skin, and be vigilant for any signs of retained shed, which can constrict circulation and lead to health issues.

Other physical indicators to monitor include the condition of your reptile's eyes, oral health, respiratory function, limb and joint health, cloacal area, and overall cleanliness. Clear, bright eyes with no signs of cloudiness or discharge are indicative of eye health. The oral cavity should be examined for any signs of mouth rot, which can manifest as redness, swelling, or discharge around the mouth. Regular, quiet breathing without wheezing, gasping, or labored breathing is a sign of healthy respiratory function.

Behavioral indicators are equally important in assessing your reptile's well-being.

A reptile's activity level can vary by species and time of day, but consistent lethargy, inactivity, or reluctance to move may signal health problems. Active exploration, basking, and hunting behaviors are indicative of wellbeing. Changes in appetite or feeding behavior can be early indicators of illness. Monitor your reptile's willingness to eat, any changes in dietary preferences, and the frequency of feedings.

If you house multiple reptiles together, observe their social interactions. Aggressive or territorial behaviors can lead to stress and health issues. Ensure that group dynamics are harmonious to prevent unnecessary stress for your reptiles. Reptiles may hide occasionally, especially during shedding or when feeling stressed. However, excessive hiding, unusual postures, or repetitive behaviors like head bobbing or pacing can indicate distress or illness.

Other behavioral indicators to consider include breeding behaviors (if applicable), response to handling, basking and thermoregulation behaviors, and response to environmental enrichment. Changes in your reptile's response to handling can provide insights into their health. If a typically docile reptile becomes aggressive or resists handling, it may be experiencing discomfort or pain. Proper thermoregulation, including regular basking, is essential for maintaining their body temperature.

In addition to monitoring your reptile's physical and behavioral indicators, consider the environmental factors within their enclosure. Proper temperature and humidity levels are essential for reptile health. Monitor and maintain the temperature gradients and humidity as per your reptile's species-specific requirements. Regular cleanliness, proper lighting, appropriate substrate, and environmental enrichment are all important aspects of reptile husbandry that can influence their health.

While recognizing physical and behavioral indicators of health is crucial, regular veterinary check-ups are equally essential for maintaining your reptile's wellbeing. Reptiles often hide illnesses until they become advanced, making professional assessments vital for early detection and treatment. A reptile-experienced veterinarian can perform thorough physical examinations, conduct diagnostic tests, and provide valuable guidance on nutrition and husbandry. These regular visits can help address health issues promptly and ensure your reptile's long and healthy life.

Conducting regular wellness assessments

Caring for a pet reptile is a unique and rewarding experience that comes with distinct responsibilities. Beyond providing the right habitat and proper diet, conducting regular wellness assessments is a fundamental aspect of proactive reptile care. These assessments allow you to monitor your reptile's health, catch potential issues early, and provide necessary adjustments to their care routine. Regular wellness assessments are essential for maintaining your reptile's health and preventing potential problems. Reptiles often hide signs of illness until they become advanced, making early detection through routine checks vital. These assessments also allow you to track your reptile's overall condition and growth over time, ensuring they are thriving in their environment.

By conducting regular wellness assessments, you can

address health issues promptly, prevent the spread of diseases, and ultimately enhance your reptile's quality of life. Early detection is crucial, as many health problems in reptiles can progress rapidly. Preventive care is another significant benefit of wellness assessments. Your veterinarian can recommend vaccinations (if applicable), parasite control, and dietary adjustments to maintain optimal health.

Behavioral insights are another valuable aspect of wellness assessments. Monitoring your reptile's behavior can reveal changes that serve as early indicators of health issues. It's essential to observe alterations in activity levels, feeding habits, social interactions, and basking behavior. These changes can provide valuable insights into your reptile's well-being.

Husbandry adjustments are an integral part of reptile care, and regular wellness assessments help identify when habitat changes or dietary modifications are needed. Your veterinarian can provide guidance on proper nutrition and supplementation, ensuring your pet receives essential nutrients for their species.

In addition to physical assessments, environmental factors within your reptile's enclosure play a crucial role in their health.

Conducting a thorough environmental assessment is part of the wellness process. Review conditions, including temperature gradients, humidity levels, lighting, substrate, and environmental enrichment. It's essential to ensure that the habitat meets the specific requirements of your reptile's species.

Fecal examinations are an important component of wellness assessments. They help identify the presence of internal parasites, and your veterinarian may recommend periodic screenings. Blood tests may also be necessary, depending on your reptile's species and health history. These tests assess various parameters, including organ function, calcium levels, and overall health.

Radiography (X-rays) and ultrasonography are diagnostic tools that your veterinarian may employ during wellness assessments. Radiography can be used to examine the skeletal structure, detect abnormalities, or assess reproductive health in sexually mature reptiles. Ultrasonography is valuable for evaluating reproductive organs, identifying eggs, and assessing internal health without invasive procedures.

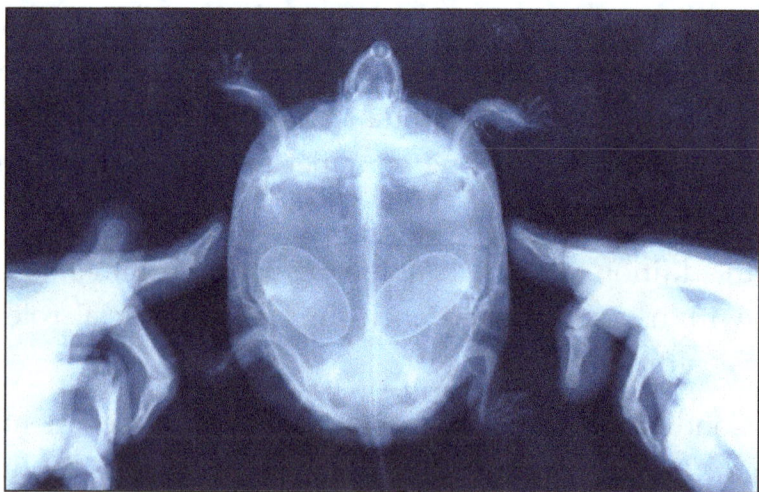

Regular discussions with your veterinarian are essential components of wellness assessments. They provide an opportunity to ask questions, seek clarification, and receive professional guidance on husbandry, habitat setup, and preventative care specific to your reptile's needs.

The frequency of wellness assessments may vary based on your reptile's age, species, and overall health. Generally, annual assessments are recommended for adult reptiles. Juvenile reptiles, which are growing rapidly, may benefit from more frequent assessments, such as every six months. Reproductive or breeding reptiles may require additional assessments during the breeding season to monitor their reproductive health.

Maintaining records of your reptile's health history is crucial for successful wellness assessments. Keep detailed records of their diet, shedding, behavior, and any past illnesses or treatments. These records can provide valuable information during assessments.

Observing your reptile's behavior regularly is also essential. Report any changes to your veterinarian, as behavioral observations can provide early indications of health issues. Proper husbandry is a critical aspect of reptile care. Ensure that your reptile's enclosure is well-maintained and meets their specific needs regarding temperature, humidity, lighting, and environmental enrichment.

Transporting your reptile safely is vital if you need to take them to the veterinarian's office for an assessment. Use an appropriate carrier or container to ensure their security and comfort during transportation.

Be prepared to ask questions and seek clarification during the assessment. Your veterinarian can provide guidance on how to improve your reptile's care, and your compliance with their advice is essential for your reptile's well-being.

Conducting regular wellness assessments for your pet reptile is a fundamental aspect of responsible ownership. These assessments allow you to monitor your reptile's health, detect potential issues early, and ensure that they are thriving in their environment. By working closely with a reptile-experienced veterinarian and following a well-established wellness schedule, you can provide the best possible care for your scaly companion. Regular assessments, coupled with attentive care and proper husbandry, contribute to a long and healthy life for your reptile.

Using Wellness Checks to Detect Early Signs of Illness in Reptiles

Regular wellness checks for your reptile are a crucial component of responsible pet ownership. Beyond providing a habitat that mimics their natural environment and ensuring a proper diet, conducting routine wellness assessments allows you to monitor your reptile's health and identify early signs of illness. Early detection is particularly important in reptiles since they often mask symptoms until an illness has progressed. In this comprehensive guide, we will dive into the significance of wellness checks and how they can help you detect early signs of illness in your scaly companion.

Reptiles, like all living creatures, can experience health issues that may not be immediately apparent. Unlike mammals, reptiles may not display overt signs of illness, such as coughing or sneezing, making it challenging for owners to identify when something is wrong. This is where wellness checks come into play. These routine assessments provide a structured approach to evaluating your reptile's overall health, often uncovering subtle signs of illness that might otherwise go unnoticed.

A typical wellness check for reptiles includes a physical examination by a reptile experienced veterinarian. During this examination, the veterinarian assesses various aspects of your reptile's health. This includes examining their body condition, skin and scales, eyes, mouth, limbs, cloacal area, and overall cleanliness. Any deviations from the norm can serve as indicators of underlying health issues.

One of the essential elements of a wellness check is the evaluation of body condition. A healthy reptile should have a well-proportioned body with no visible ribs or bones protruding. This assessment helps detect changes in weight, which could be indicative of various health problems, such as malnutrition, organ dysfunction, or parasites.

The condition of your reptile's skin and scales is another vital aspect of the physical examination. A healthy reptile should have smooth, vibrant, and well-hydrated skin. Dry, flaky, or discolored skin may suggest dehydration, shedding issues, or underlying health concerns. The examination also involves checking for any abnormalities in skin texture, color, or pigmentation.

The eyes are windows to a reptile's overall health. During a wellness check, the veterinarian assesses the eyes for any signs of cloudiness, swelling, discharge, or unusual pigmentation. Clear, bright eyes are indicative of good eye health, while sunken or closed eyes may signal dehydration or an underlying problem.

The examination extends to your reptile's oral cavity, where the health of their mouth and gums is assessed. Signs of mouth rot, which can manifest as redness, swelling, or discharge around the mouth, are carefully examined. Additionally, the gums and teeth are checked for any abnormalities that may require attention.

Respiratory function is another critical aspect of a wellness check. Your reptile's breathing should be regular and unlabored, without any wheezing or gasping. Respiratory distress may suggest respiratory infections or other health issues that need further investigation.

Limbs and joints are examined for signs of swelling, stiffness, or lameness. Proper limb function is essential for your reptile's mobility and overall well-being. Any abnormalities in limb movement can provide clues about underlying issues.

The cloacal area, where reptiles excrete waste and, in some species, lay eggs, is also subject to examination. Changes in this area, such as swelling, discoloration, or discharge, can be indicative of reproductive or urinary issues that require attention.

Aside from the physical examination, wellness checks also encompass evaluating your reptile's behavior and activity level. Changes in your reptile's activity level can vary by species and time of day but consistent lethargy, inactivity, or reluctance to move may signal health problems. On the other hand, active exploration, basking, and hunting behaviors are indicative of well-being.

Monitoring your reptile's appetite and feeding habits is an integral part of a wellness check. Changes in appetite or feeding behavior can be early indicators of illness. This involves assessing their willingness to eat, any shifts in dietary preferences, and the frequency of feedings.

Social interactions among reptiles, particularly if you house multiple reptiles together, are observed to ensure harmonious group dynamics. Aggressive or territorial behaviors can lead to stress and health issues among reptiles.

Unusual behaviors, such as excessive hiding, peculiar postures, or repetitive actions like head bobbing or pacing, are also considered during wellness checks. While reptiles may hide occasionally, excessive hiding, unusual postures, or repetitive behaviors can indicate distress or illness that merits further investigation.

Reptiles rely on external heat sources for thermoregulation, and wellness checks involve monitoring their basking and thermoregulation behaviors. Proper thermoregulation is essential for maintaining their body temperature, and prolonged avoidance of basking spots may suggest issues with temperature regulation or environmental conditions.

The response to handling can also provide insights into your reptile's health. Changes in their response, such as increased aggression or resistance to handling, may be indicators of discomfort or pain.

Environmental factors within your reptile's enclosure are critical to their wellbeing. As part of wellness assessments, the conditions within the enclosure are reviewed, including temperature gradients, humidity levels, lighting, substrate, and environmental enrichment. Ensuring that the habitat meets the specific requirements of your reptile's species is essential for their overall health.

Regular cleanliness of the enclosure is emphasized during wellness checks. Keeping the habitat clean and free from waste buildup is crucial to preventing the accumulation of harmful bacteria or parasites.

Wellness checks are an integral part of responsible reptile ownership, as they allow for the early detection of health issues. Reptiles have evolved to hide signs of illness, making it challenging for owners to identify problems without professional assistance. Routine wellness checks provide a structured and comprehensive approach to assessing your reptile's health, encompassing both physical and behavioral aspects.

In addition to the visual and behavioral assessments, your reptile-experienced veterinarian may recommend diagnostic tests as part of a wellness check. These tests may include fecal examinations to detect the presence of internal parasites, blood tests to assess organ function and overall health, radiography (X-rays) to examine the skeletal structure and detect abnormalities, and ultrasonography to evaluate reproductive organs and internal health without invasive procedures.

Regular wellness checks also offer an opportunity to discuss your reptile's care and husbandry with your veterinarian. They can provide guidance on nutrition, habitat setup, and preventative measures tailored to your reptile's specific needs.

The frequency of wellness checks may vary depending on your reptile's age, species, and overall health. Typically, annual wellness checks are recommended for adult reptiles. Juvenile reptiles, which undergo rapid growth and development, may benefit from more frequent assessments, such as every six months.

Reproductive or breeding reptiles may require additional assessments during the breeding season to monitor reproductive health and address any issues related to egg-laying.

To prepare for wellness checks, maintaining detailed records of your reptile's health history is essential. Keep records of their diet, shedding, behavior, and any past illnesses or treatments. These records can provide valuable information during assessments.

Regularly observing your reptile's behavior and reporting any changes to your veterinarian is crucial, as behavioral observations can provide early indications of health issues. Proper husbandry is a cornerstone of reptile care, so ensure that your reptile's enclosure is well-maintained and meets their specific requirements in terms of temperature, humidity, lighting, and environmental enrichment.

Common Health Issues and Their Treatments

An In-Depth Examination of Common Health Problems in Reptiles

Caring for reptiles entails more than providing the right

habitat and nutrition; it also involves vigilant monitoring for common health problems that can affect these unique creatures. Unlike mammals, reptiles often mask symptoms of illness until they become advanced, making it essential for owners to be aware of the potential issues that may arise. In this in-depth examination, we will explore some of the most common health problems in reptiles, including respiratory infections, parasitic infestations, and other concerns that reptile owners should be well-informed about.

Respiratory Infections

Respiratory infections are among the most prevalent health issues in reptiles. These infections can be caused by various factors, including improper husbandry, such as inadequate temperature and humidity levels, or exposure to drafts. Common signs of respiratory infections in reptiles include labored breathing, wheezing, nasal discharge, and open-mouth breathing. In severe cases, affected reptiles may exhibit lethargy and loss of appetite.

Respiratory infections can affect the upper respiratory tract (URT) or lower respiratory tract (LRT) of reptiles. URT infections are often associated with nasal discharge and sneezing, while LRT infections can lead to more severe symptoms, including pneumonia. Prompt veterinary intervention is crucial when a respiratory infection is suspected, as untreated infections can progress and lead to serious health complications.

Parasitic Infestations

Parasitic infestations are another common health concern in reptiles. Internal parasites, such as nematodes, cestodes, and protozoa, can affect various organs, including the gastrointestinal tract, liver, and lungs. External parasites like mites and ticks can also afflict reptiles, causing skin irritation, scales, and shell damage.

The symptoms of parasitic infestations can vary depending on the type of parasite and the affected organ system. Reptiles with internal parasites may display signs such as regurgitation, diarrhea, weight loss, and lethargy. External parasites can cause visible skin abnormalities and discomfort.

Preventative measures, such as maintaining a clean enclosure and regularly disinfecting your reptile's habitat, can help reduce the risk of parasitic infestations. Routine fecal examinations and wellness checks by a reptile-experienced veterinarian can aid in early detection and treatment.

Metabolic Bone Disease (MBD)

Metabolic Bone Disease is a common ailment in reptiles, particularly those with inadequate calcium intake or improper exposure to UVB lighting. MBD results from a calcium imbalance, leading to weakened bones and deformities. Signs of MBD include soft or misshapen shells in turtles and tortoises, weak limbs, tremors, and difficulty moving.

To prevent MBD, reptiles require access to calcium supplements and exposure to UVB lighting to support proper calcium absorption. A balanced diet, including calcium-rich foods, is essential. If MBD is suspected, a veterinarian can recommend treatment options to correct calcium imbalances and improve the reptile's bone health.

Dehydration

Dehydration is a common health concern, particularly in arid-dwelling reptiles. Inadequate access to water, high temperatures, or low humidity levels can contribute to dehydration. Signs of dehydration may include sunken eyes, wrinkled or flaky skin, lethargy, and reduced appetite.

Proper hydration is crucial for maintaining the health of reptiles. Ensure that your reptile has access to clean, fresh water at all times and adjust humidity levels and temperature gradients as needed. Dehydrated reptiles may require rehydration therapy administered by a veterinarian.

Stress and Behavioral Issues

Reptiles can experience stress and behavioral issues, often as a result of improper husbandry or handling. Stress can manifest in various ways, including changes in behavior, appetite, or activity level. Behavioral issues can include aggression, excessive hiding, and repetitive actions.

To mitigate stress and behavioral problems, it's essential to provide a suitable habitat, including proper hiding places and environmental enrichment. Minimize disturbances and handle your reptile with care and gentleness. If stress-related behaviors persist, consult with a veterinarian or reptile behavior specialist for guidance.

Egg-Binding

Female reptiles that reproduce through egg-laying are susceptible to a condition known as egg-binding, where eggs become trapped within the reproductive tract and cannot be laid. Symptoms of egg-binding include lethargy, swelling of the abdomen, and straining. Left untreated, egg-binding can be life-threatening.

Prompt veterinary intervention is crucial for reptiles experiencing egg-binding.

Treatment may include providing supplemental heat, hydration, and supportive care to assist in egg passage. In some cases, surgery may be necessary to remove eggs that cannot be passed naturally.

Dermatological Issues

Reptiles can develop various dermatological issues, including skin infections, fungal or bacterial growth, and shell rot. These problems are often linked to poor habitat conditions, such as inadequate humidity levels or unsanitary enclosures. Signs may include changes in skin texture, color, or lesions on the skin or shell.

Proper husbandry, maintaining clean habitats, and monitoring humidity levels can help prevent dermatological issues. When detected early, these issues can often be treated with topical or systemic medications prescribed by a veterinarian.

Administering medications and providing supportive care

Administering medications and providing supportive care for reptiles are crucial aspects of reptile healthcare, and they require a thoughtful approach due to the unique nature of these creatures. Unlike mammals, reptiles possess distinct physiological characteristics, which must be considered when administering medications or offering supportive care. This detailed guide will delve into the factors to consider when providing medical treatment and support for your reptilian companion.

Administering medications to reptiles necessitates a gentle touch and precise techniques. The choice of medication delivery method depends on factors such as the reptile's size, species, and the type of medication prescribed.

Oral medications are often given directly from a syringe or dropper. Some reptiles can be trained to accept oral medications this way, while others may require the medication to be mixed with a palatable food item, such as a favorite fruit or insect. It's vital to ensure that the medication is fully consumed to guarantee the correct dosage.

Injections, such as intramuscular (IM) or subcutaneous (SC) injections, may be necessary for specific medications or health conditions. These should be administered by a trained veterinarian to minimize stress and potential complications.

Topical medications, like creams, ointments, or topical solutions, can be applied directly to affected areas of the skin or shell for dermatological issues. Proper application following your veterinarian's instructions is essential to ensure that the medication is not ingested.

Nebulization therapy may be recommended for respiratory issues. It involves using a nebulizer to create a fine mist of medication, which the reptile inhales. This method can be effective in treating respiratory infections.

Supportive care is an integral part of the recovery process for sick or injured reptiles. It involves providing additional care and attention to address the specific needs of the individual and aid in their recuperation.

Isolation of sick reptiles is essential to prevent the potential spread of diseases to healthy reptiles. The isolation enclosure should maintain appropriate temperature and humidity levels.

Maintaining proper hydration is crucial for sick reptiles. Some may require supplemental fluids, which can be administered orally or through injection under veterinary guidance. Always ensure that clean water is readily available.

Nutrition should be tailored to the reptile's condition. Some sick reptiles may require a temporary shift to a softer or more digestible diet. Hand-feeding may be necessary for those with a reduced appetite.

Temperature and humidity levels within the enclosure should be maintained appropriately. Sick reptiles often benefit from slightly elevated temperatures to support their immune system and metabolism.

Minimizing stressors in the environment, such as loud noises, excessive handling, or sudden changes in lighting, is essential. A quiet and stress-free environment promotes healing.

Regular monitoring of the reptile's condition, including their behavior, appetite, and any changes in symptoms, is crucial. Keeping a record of observations will aid in follow-up appointments with the veterinarian.

Rehabilitation, when necessary, should be gradual. After recovering from an illness or injury, provide a slow return to normal activities and routines. Some reptiles may require rehabilitation exercises to regain strength and mobility.

Veterinary guidance is paramount throughout the process. Always follow your veterinarian's instructions regarding medications, treatments, and supportive care. Consult with a reptile-experienced veterinarian for tailored advice.

Administering medications and providing supportive care for reptiles can present unique challenges. These animals are known for their resistance to handling and may become stressed during medical procedures. Precise dosage calculations are crucial, as reptiles can be sensitive to medications.

Anesthesia or sedation may be necessary for certain procedures, and these should only be administered by qualified professionals. Maintaining hygiene and cleanliness throughout the medication and supportive care process is vital.

Preventative Measures for Maintaining Optimal Health in Reptiles

Ensuring the optimal health of your reptilian companion involves a proactive approach that emphasizes preventative measures. Preventative care is essential to help reptiles thrive and avoid common health issues that may arise due to improper husbandry or environmental conditions. In this comprehensive guide, we will explore the key preventative measures that reptile owners should implement to maintain their pet's wellbeing.

Proper habitat setup is paramount to a reptile's health. Research and understand the specific requirements of your reptile's species, including temperature gradients, humidity levels, lighting, and enclosure size. Provide a suitable substrate that mimics their natural environment and allows for proper burrowing or basking.

Regularly clean and sanitize the enclosure to prevent the buildup of harmful bacteria or parasites. Ensure that all components, such as heating elements and lighting fixtures, are functioning correctly and safely.

Maintaining proper hydration is critical for reptiles. Always provide access to clean, fresh water in a shallow dish that allows easy access for drinking and soaking. Some reptiles, like chameleons, may prefer water droplets on leaves for drinking. Monitor water levels daily to ensure your reptile has an adequate supply.

A balanced diet is crucial for reptile health. Research the dietary preferences and nutritional needs of your specific species. Provide a variety of prey items or plant matter to meet their dietary requirements. Consider calcium and vitamin supplements, as some reptiles require additional supplementation.

Avoid overfeeding or offering inappropriate foods that may lead to obesity or nutritional imbalances. Consult with a reptile experienced veterinarian for guidance on proper nutrition.

Reptiles often require exposure to UVB lighting to metabolize calcium and maintain proper bone health. Ensure that your reptile's enclosure has appropriate UVB lighting fixtures. Follow manufacturer guidelines for bulb replacement, as UVB output diminishes over time.

Position the lighting fixture at the correct distance to provide the necessary UVB exposure without causing harm. Monitor UVB levels with a reliable UVB meter to ensure consistency.

Reptiles are ectothermic, relying on external heat sources to regulate their body temperature. Maintain proper temperature gradients within the enclosure, allowing your reptile to thermoregulate effectively. Use thermostats and thermometers to monitor temperature levels accurately.

Provide basking spots with appropriate heat sources,

such as heat lamps or heating pads, to allow your reptile to achieve their desired body temperature. Ensure that there are cooler areas within the enclosure for your reptile to retreat to when needed.

Reptiles have diverse humidity requirements based on their species. Research and maintain the appropriate humidity levels for your reptile's specific needs. Utilize humidity gauges to monitor humidity accurately.

For reptiles requiring higher humidity, misting the enclosure or providing a humidity box can help maintain the necessary moisture levels. Conversely, reptiles needing lower humidity should have well-ventilated enclosures.

Reptiles benefit from environmental enrichment to stimulate natural behaviors and mental activity. Provide hiding places, climbing structures, and items for exploration.

Change the arrangement of objects periodically to prevent boredom.

When introducing a new reptile to your collection, implement quarantine procedures to prevent the potential spread of diseases. Quarantine the new reptile in a separate enclosure for 1- 2 months while monitoring for any signs of illness.

Schedule regular wellness checks with a reptile-experienced veterinarian, even when your reptile appears healthy. Annual checkups are recommended for adult reptiles, while juveniles or those with health concerns may require more frequent visits.

Wellness checks include physical examinations, fecal examinations, and blood tests to assess your reptile's overall health. They also provide an opportunity to discuss husbandry practices and preventative care measures.

Reptiles can become stressed if overhandled. Minimize unnecessary handling and provide hiding spots or shelters where your reptile can retreat when feeling stressed. Respect their need for solitude and minimize disruptions to their environment.

Continuously educate yourself about your reptile's species-specific needs, behaviors, and potential health concerns. Stay updated on advancements in reptile care and seek guidance from reputable sources, including veterinarians and experienced reptile enthusiasts.

Chapter 6

Reproduction and Breeding

Reptile reproduction varies greatly among species, with some laying eggs and others giving birth to live young. Typically, reptiles reproduce sexually, with males fertilizing the eggs internally or externally. Breeding usually requires creating appropriate conditions for nesting or mating, such as temperature and humidity regulation. Careful monitoring is essential during the reproductive process, and newly hatched or born reptiles often require specific care to ensure their survival. It's crucial to research the specific reproductive behavior and needs of your reptile species before attempting to breed them, as it varies widely among different types of reptiles.

Understanding Reproductive Behaviors

Detailed examination of mating rituals and courtship behaviors

Mating rituals and courtship behaviors in reptiles are fascinating and diverse, varying greatly among different species. These rituals are essential for successful reproduction and are often influenced by environmental factors, hormonal changes, and individual behaviors. In this in-depth exploration, we will delve into the intricacies of reptile courtship behaviors and the fascinating rituals that lead to successful mating.

Many reptiles, such as chameleons and anoles, employ vivid color changes and body language to communicate their intentions during courtship. Males often display vibrant colors and engage in conspicuous body postures to attract females. These displays can signal readiness for mating and may also serve to establish dominance over rival males.

Some reptile species engage in vocalizations and calls as part of their courtship behavior. Male frogs, for example, are known for their distinctive mating calls, which can be heard during the breeding season. These calls serve to attract females and establish territory. Each species has its unique vocalization patterns and sounds.

Reptiles, particularly snakes and lizards, use chemical signals called pheromones to communicate their readiness for mating. These pheromones are released by glands and can be detected by potential mates. Females can follow these chemical trails to locate males or assess their suitability as mates.

Some reptiles engage in intricate courtship dances and rituals. For instance, male turtles may swim around females, bobbing their heads and performing underwater displays to demonstrate their interest. These dances can be highly synchronized and involve specific movements that signal readiness for mating.

In some reptile species, males offer gifts to females as part of their courtship. Male lizards, for example, may present prey items, such as insects, to females. This behavior not only showcases the male's hunting prowess but also provides nourishment for the female, potentially influencing her decision to mate.

Males of certain reptile species engage in physical combat or displays of dominance to compete for the attention of females. These confrontations can be intense and may involve pushing, wrestling, or biting. The victorious male often gains the opportunity to mate with the female.

Courtship behaviors can vary in duration and persistence. Some reptiles engage in prolonged courtship rituals, while others have brief and intense interactions. The length and intensity of courtship can depend on factors like environmental conditions, female receptivity, and the competition among males.

In some reptile species, males provide nuptial gifts or engage in nuptial feeding during courtship. These offerings can include prey items or other resources that benefit the female. Nuptial feeding is thought to enhance the female's reproductive fitness and may influence her choice of mate.

Reptiles exhibit a wide range of mating positions and behaviors. Some species engage in copulatory locking, where the male and female become physically connected during mating. Others may adopt specific body positions or tail-arching behaviors to facilitate copulation.

In certain reptile species, both males and females may have multiple mating partners during a breeding season. This behavior can lead to competition among males and promiscuity among females. The outcome of multiple matings can influence genetic diversity within a population.

Understanding the intricacies of mating rituals and courtship behaviors in reptiles is essential for those interested in breeding or studying these remarkable creatures. Each species has evolved unique strategies to ensure successful reproduction, often adapted to their specific ecological niches and environmental conditions. Observing and researching these behaviors not only enhances our knowledge of reptile biology but also deepens our appreciation for their complex and diverse natural histories.

Recognizing Signs of Readiness for Breeding in Reptiles

Breeding in reptiles is a complex process that often relies on specific behavioral, physiological, and environmental cues. To successfully breed reptiles, it's essential to recognize the signs of readiness for breeding in both males and females. These signs can vary among species, but several common indicators can help reptile enthusiasts and breeders determine when their reptiles are prepared for mating.

Many reptile species exhibit seasonal changes in behavior and physiology that signal their readiness for breeding. These changes often coincide with environmental factors such as temperature, humidity, and daylight length. During the breeding season, males may become more active, territorial, and display courtship behaviors, while females may exhibit changes in appetite, activity level, and receptivity to males.

Males of many reptile species become more active and exploratory when they are ready to breed. They may roam their enclosures in search of potential mates or engage in territorial behaviors, such as patrolling specific areas. Increased activity can be an early sign of readiness for breeding.

One of the most obvious signs of readiness for breeding in males is the display of courtship behaviors. These behaviors can include vibrant color changes, body postures, head-bobbing, and other visual displays. Courtship rituals are intended to attract females and communicate the male's intentions.

Some reptiles and amphibians engage in vocalizations or calls as part of their courtship. Male frogs, for example, emit distinctive mating calls that can be heard during the breeding season. These calls serve to attract females and establish territory, signalling readiness for mating.

Reptiles often release chemical signals called pheromones to communicate their readiness for breeding. These pheromones can be detected by potential mates, particularly in species with a keen sense of smell. Females may follow these pheromone trails to locate males, while males may use pheromones to signal their presence and intentions.

The physical condition of a reptile can be indicative of readiness for breeding. Males may exhibit enhanced muscular development and body mass, while females may display changes in abdominal size or shape. Observing these physical changes can provide insights into their reproductive status.

Some reptiles may experience changes in appetite and feeding behavior as they prepare for breeding. Females may reduce their food intake, diverting energy towards egg production. In contrast, males may become more focused on foraging to maintain their energy levels during the mating season.

Female reptiles often undergo physiological changes in preparation for breeding. These changes can include the development of follicles, ovulation, and the production of eggs. In some species, these changes may be visible through palpation or ultrasound imaging.

Observing the interactions between potential mating partners is crucial. Males may initiate courtship behaviors, while females may either accept or reject their advances. Recognizing the cues and responses of both males and females during these interactions is essential for successful breeding.

Reptiles in captivity may require specific environmental cues to trigger readiness for breeding. These cues can include changes in temperature, humidity, and light cycles. Providing appropriate environmental stimulation can help replicate natural breeding conditions.

Temperature and photoperiod (daylight length) play significant roles in triggering breeding behavior in reptiles. Some species require specific temperature changes to induce reproductive activity. Manipulating these factors in captivity can simulate seasonal cues and prompt readiness for breeding. For instance, one method used by reptile owners to initiate breeding behavior is by mimicking natural seasonal changes through temperature adjustments. This includes inducing brumation, a period where reptiles respond to colder temperatures, such as in winter, by slowing down their body systems. This natural slowing down serves as a signal to the reptile's body that warmer temperatures are approaching, indicating the imminent arrival of the breeding season.

Understanding the signs of readiness for breeding in reptiles is essential for successful captive breeding programs and responsible reptile ownership. However, it's important to note that these signs can vary widely among species, so thorough research and speciesspecific knowledge are crucial. Additionally, ethical breeding practices should prioritize the health and welfare of the reptiles involved, ensuring their well-being throughout the breeding process.

Species-Specific Variations in Reproductive Strategies in Reptiles

Reptiles, encompassing a wide range of species across

various ecosystems, exhibit a remarkable diversity of reproductive strategies that have evolved in response to their specific ecological niches and environmental conditions. One of the fundamental distinctions in reptile reproduction lies in whether they are oviparous or viviparous.

Oviparous reptiles, which make up the majority of reptile species, lay eggs as their primary means of reproduction. Within the realm of oviparous reptiles, there exists a fascinating spectrum of adaptations. For instance, some reptiles practice guarded nesting, wherein females remain near their nests to protect their eggs from potential predators. Certain species, like sea turtles, return to specific beaches to lay their eggs, relying on the environmental cues provided by the beach's conditions for successful incubation.

Temperature-dependent sex determination (TSD) is another intriguing adaptation seen in oviparous reptiles, where the temperature at which the eggs incubate determines the sex of the offspring.

Viviparous reptiles, on the other hand, have evolved the ability to give birth to live offspring rather than laying eggs. This mode of reproduction can take various forms, with some species exhibiting placental viviparity, akin to mammals, wherein they develop specialized placental structures to nourish and provide oxygen to their embryos. Others, like certain garter snakes, retain eggs internally but still lay them as fully formed eggs, which hatch shortly before or during birth.

Intriguingly, parthenogenesis is another phenomenon observed in some reptiles, albeit rarely. This process allows females to produce offspring without fertilization by males, resulting in offspring that are typically genetically identical to the mother.

Mating and courtship behaviors among reptiles are as diverse as their reproductive patterns. While some engage in elaborate courtship rituals involving vibrant displays of colors and body postures, others may compete for mates through physical combat or dominance displays. The complexity of mating behaviors varies widely, reflecting the species' specific reproductive strategies and ecological roles.

Reptile parental care behaviors also vary significantly. While some species, such as crocodilians, exhibit extensive parental care, with mothers guarding nests and even transporting hatchlings to water, many reptiles, particularly lizards and snakes, provide no parental care beyond laying eggs or giving birth.

The differences between egg-laying and live-bearing species are among the most fundamental distinctions in reptile reproductive strategies. Egg-laying species require precise conditions for egg incubation, including suitable temperature and humidity, while live-bearing species invest more energy in embryonic development within the mother's body and give birth to fully formed offspring.

Preparing for Breeding

Creating a suitable breeding environment, including temperature and humidity control

Establishing a suitable breeding environment is crucial

for the successful reproduction of reptiles. This environment should mimic the natural conditions that the reptiles would experience in the wild, including temperature and humidity control. Proper environmental conditions are essential for the health and well-being of both the parent reptiles and their offspring.

Temperature control is a fundamental aspect of creating a suitable breeding environment for reptiles. Different reptile species have specific temperature requirements, which can vary significantly. It's essential to research the preferred temperature range for your particular species and provide a gradient within their enclosure to allow for thermoregulation.

Most reptiles require a basking area with a heat source that provides a temperature at the upper end of their preferred range. This allows them to thermoregulate by moving between warmer and cooler areas in the

enclosure. To maintain consistent temperatures, it's advisable to use thermostats in conjunction with heating devices like heat lamps, ceramic heaters, or heating pads. Thermostats help prevent overheating or temperature fluctuations. Many reptiles benefit from a slight temperature drop during the night, simulating natural conditions. This nighttime drop can be achieved by reducing the intensity of heat sources or using heating devices specifically designed for nighttime use.

Humidity control is equally vital, as it can influence breeding behavior, egg incubation, and the overall health of reptiles. The humidity requirements vary among species, and it's essential to research and replicate the specific conditions needed for your reptiles. Use hygrometers to monitor humidity levels accurately within the enclosure. This allows you to make adjustments as needed to maintain the appropriate humidity range. For species requiring higher humidity, misting systems can help maintain moisture levels. Automated misting systems can be programmed to release a fine mist at specific intervals, ensuring consistent humidity. Selecting an appropriate substrate can also influence humidity levels. Substrates like coconut coir or sphagnum moss can help retain moisture and create a suitable microclimate. Providing hide boxes with dampened substrates inside can serve as microenvironments with higher humidity, which some reptiles, particularly egg-laying females, may require. If breeding reptiles that lay eggs, consider using separate incubation chambers with controlled temperature and humidity settings. This allows precise control over incubation conditions, increasing the chances of successful hatching.

Mimicking seasonal variation in temperature and humidity, if applicable to your species, can trigger breeding behaviors. For example, replicating a dry and cooler "winter" period followed by a warmer and more humid "spring" can stimulate reproductive activity. Provide environmental enrichment to reduce stress and promote natural behaviors. This can include hiding spots, climbing structures, and visual barriers to create a more comfortable and stimulating environment for breeding reptiles. Consistently monitor temperature and humidity levels using reliable equipment. Make necessary adjustments promptly to maintain optimal conditions. Conduct thorough research on the specific temperature and humidity requirements for your reptile species. Seek guidance from experienced breeders or herpetologists familiar with your chosen species.

Selecting compatible mates and monitoring for successful copulation

The process of breeding reptiles is a meticulous endeavor that demands a careful consideration of mate compatibility and a vigilant approach to ensure successful copulation. Fundamental to this process is the selection of suitable mates and a profound understanding of their individual needs and behaviors, both of which are indispensable steps in achieving successful breeding outcomes.

Mate Compatibility holds pivotal importance in the realm of reptile breeding. It entails a comprehensive evaluation of various factors to maximize the likelihood of successful reproduction. Among these considerations, the foremost is Species Compatibility, wherein the importance of conspecific pairings cannot be overstated. Attempting to crossbreed different species can lead to a plethora of issues, ranging from health complications to the production of infertile offspring.

Age and size of potential mates are equally critical aspects to contemplate. In certain reptile species, significant disparities in size between partners can give rise to difficulties during copulation or elevate the risk of injuries. Consequently, it is generally advisable to pair individuals of similar sizes and ages.

The health and genetics of prospective mates must not

be overlooked. Opting for mates that are in optimal health and devoid of known genetic defects or diseases is paramount. Breeding individuals with underlying health issues can result in compromised offspring or the inadvertent transmission of diseases.

Behavioral compatibility serves as an essential criterion for mate selection. Observing the behavior of potential mates is an indispensable exercise. Ensuring that they exhibit normal courtship behaviors and manifest mutual interest in one another is crucial to fostering successful breeding.

Once compatible mates are carefully chosen, the next crucial step is monitoring for successful copulation. Different reptile species often display an array of courtship and mating behaviors, necessitating a thorough understanding of these behaviors for effective monitoring.

Courting behaviors characteristic of each specific reptile species should be meticulously studied. It's common for males to engage in various courtship displays, such as head-bobbing, color changes, or vocalizations, as a means to attract females. Paying close attention to these behaviors can provide invaluable early indications of interest and readiness for copulation.

Successful copulation hinges on the physical interactions between the male and female. These interactions may include mounting, tail-straddling, and other speciesspecific behaviors. Careful observation of these actions is essential to confirm the occurrence of copulation.

Furthermore, the duration and frequency of copulation

attempts can vary significantly among different reptile species.

While some may engage in prolonged copulation sessions, others may exhibit shorter, intermittent interactions. Monitoring the frequency and duration of copulation attempts is essential to assess mating success accurately.

Post-copulation behavior is another facet of monitoring. After copulation, observing any alterations in the behavior or interactions between the mating pair is paramount. In some species, males may become more protective or defensive of the female following successful copulation, offering additional insight into the breeding process.

In certain cases, visual confirmation of copulation may be necessary, along with monitoring for the presence of sperm plugs or mating plugs, which serve as physical indicators of successful mating in specific reptile species.

Detailed documentation of observations, including dates, times, and behaviors exhibited by the mating pair, is invaluable for tracking breeding attempts and predicting potential hatching dates. Keeping meticulous records aids in maintaining a comprehensive breeding history.

While monitoring is crucial, it is equally vital to provide the mating pair with privacy and minimize disturbances. Excessive handling or disruptions can lead to stress and potentially disrupt the breeding process, underscoring the importance of allowing the reptiles their necessary space.

Lastly, in cases where copulation is not immediately successful, patience is key. It may be necessary to allow the pair to attempt mating multiple times, as some reptile species require several copulation sessions for fertilization to occur.

The role of diet and nutritional preparation for breeding reptiles

Diet and nutritional preparation are fundamental elements in the successful breeding of reptiles. These aspects are essential not only for the health and well-being of the breeding individuals but also for the development of healthy offspring. The diversity among reptile species necessitates an understanding of their specific dietary requirements to ensure they are in optimal breeding condition.

Reptiles have distinctive nutritional requirements, which vary from one species to another. It is imperative to comprehend these requirements, particularly during the breeding season, to support successful reproduction. Certain key nutrients play critical roles:

Protein is of utmost importance, especially for females preparing to lay eggs. Adequate protein intake is essential for egg development, embryo growth, and overall reproductive health. Different reptile species may have varying protein requirements, with insectivorous species often needing higher protein levels during breeding.

Calcium is another vital nutrient, particularly crucial for egg-laying reptiles. It is necessary for the development of eggshells and muscle contractions during egg-laying. Calcium supplementation is often recommended for breeding females to prevent issues such as egg-binding.

Vitamins and minerals, including Vitamin D, are integral to reptile nutrition. Vitamin D is essential for calcium absorption, and reptiles relying on UVB lighting for vitamin D synthesis should have access to appropriate lighting.

The period leading up to the breeding season is crucial for both male and female reptiles. Female reptiles need to be in optimal physical condition, with sufficient fat reserves to support egg development. Overweight females may experience difficulties in reproduction, while underweight females may lack the energy required for egg-laying. Similarly, males benefit from pre-breeding nutritional preparation to ensure they are physically fit for successful copulation.

Feeding schedules should be established to meet the specific needs of breeding reptiles. Factors like species, age, and individual requirements should be considered:

The frequency of feedings may increase for some reptiles during the breeding season to provide extra energy and nutrients. However, monitoring body condition is vital to prevent overfeeding.

Feeding quantities should be adjusted to match the specific needs of breeding reptiles. Pregnant females may require larger meals to support egg development, while males may need to maintain their body condition without excessive weight gain.

Many reptile species exhibit seasonal variations in their dietary needs due to changes in temperature, photoperiod (day length), and food availability. These variations must be considered in nutritional preparation.

Some reptile species undergo hibernation or reduced feeding during the winter months. Proper nutritional preparation before hibernation is essential to ensure they enter hibernation in good condition.

As the breeding season approaches, reptiles may experience increased activity and energy expenditure. Their diet should reflect these changes, focusing on providing the necessary nutrients for reproduction.

Offering a diverse diet is essential to meet the nutritional requirements of reptiles. Replicating the variety of prey items and vegetation that wild reptiles consume is key to achieving a balanced diet.

Insectivorous reptiles should be provided with a variety of insects, while herbivorous species require a selection of leafy greens, vegetables, and fruits. Omnivorous reptiles need both animal and plant matter in their diet.

Supplements, such as calcium powder with or without vitamin D3 and multivitamin supplements, are often used to ensure reptiles receive essential vitamins and minerals. The use of supplements should be guided by a veterinarian or an experienced reptile keeper to avoid over-supplementation.

Proper hydration is crucial for all reptiles, especially during the breeding season. Pregnant females may require increased hydration to support egg development. Access to fresh, clean water and the provision of a shallow dish for soaking, if needed, help reptiles regulate their hydration levels.

After breeding, continued nutritional care is essential. Females may require additional nutrients for egg production and pregnancy, while males benefit from ongoing nutritional support for overall health.

Care for Pregnant Reptiles and Their Offspring

Providing appropriate nesting sites and conditions

Creating suitable nesting sites and conditions is a critical aspect of successful breeding for many reptile species. These sites not only serve as safe locations for egg deposition but also play a crucial role in ensuring the health and survival of offspring.

The first step in providing appropriate nesting sites and conditions is to understand the specific nesting requirements of the reptile species in question. Different reptiles have varying preferences and these preferences are influenced by factors such as habitat, behavior, and reproductive biology.

Nesting requirements include considerations like the type of nesting substrate preferred by the species, the depth at which eggs are buried, nesting temperature, and the location of nesting sites. For instance, some reptiles favor sandy or loamy soils, while others may opt for leaf litter or decaying vegetation as their nesting substrate. Some bury their eggs deep in the substrate, while others may only partially bury them or lay them on the surface. Temperature can influence the sex ratio of hatchlings in certain reptile species through temperature-dependent sex determination

(TSD). Nesting site location is also crucial, with reptiles choosing specific spots, such as burrows, under vegetation, or concealed locations, for nesting.

Once the nesting requirements of the species are understood, the next step is to replicate natural conditions as closely as possible within the captive environment. This involves factors such as substrate composition, temperature, humidity, and nesting site structure.

Choosing the right nesting substrate is paramount, as it should match the natural substrate of the species. Whether it's sandy soil, leaf litter, or another material, the substrate should be loose enough to allow easy excavation by the female but stable enough to support the nest. Providing nesting boxes or areas that mimic natural nesting sites can be beneficial, with options like containers filled with the appropriate substrate or designated areas within the enclosure for digging and nesting.

Maintaining the correct temperature and humidity levels in the nesting area is crucial. For species with TSD, precise temperature control during incubation is essential to ensure the desired sex ratio of hatchlings. To achieve these conditions, hygrometers and thermostats can be used. Additionally, nesting sites should offer protection from potential predators, both within and outside the enclosure, which may involve adding barriers or covers to prevent access by other animals.

Effective breeding management involves continual monitoring of nesting conditions and making necessary adjustments as the breeding season progresses. This includes regular temperature monitoring, humidity management, protection from disturbances, and awareness of the typical incubation period for the species. Detailed record-keeping aids in tracking the progress of the breeding program, helping ensure that conditions remain optimal for the reptiles and their eggs.

After egg deposition, it is essential to provide post-nesting care to ensure the health and survival of both the eggs and hatchlings. This care may involve egg collection and placement in an appropriate incubation chamber with controlled temperature and humidity settings or ensuring that the nesting site remains undisturbed until hatching occurs if the eggs are left with the female in the enclosure.

For reptiles with TSD, it may be necessary to determine the sex of hatchlings. Proper sexing is essential for keeping breeding records and managing future pairings.

Monitoring gestation periods and preparing for egg-laying

Monitoring gestation periods and preparing for egg-laying are essential aspects of reptile breeding. These processes require careful observation and proactive measures to ensure the health and safety of the pregnant female and the development of viable eggs.

Gestation periods vary widely among reptile species, and knowing the specific duration for the species in question is crucial. Some reptiles, like turtles and tortoises, have relatively long gestation periods that can span several weeks to several months, while others, such as certain snakes and lizards, may have shorter gestation periods. Accurate recordkeeping of mating dates and behavior is invaluable for predicting the timing of egglaying.

As the gestation period progresses, it's important to closely monitor the pregnant female's health and behavior. Pregnant reptiles may exhibit changes in appetite, activity levels, and body condition. Some may become more reclusive, seeking out suitable nesting sites. Observing these behavioral changes can provide valuable insights into the impending egg-laying.

Preparing for egg-laying involves creating a suitable environment for the female to deposit her eggs safely. This includes ensuring that the enclosure or nesting area provides the necessary conditions, such as temperature, humidity, and nesting substrate. The choice of substrate should match the species' preferences, whether it's sandy soil, leaf litter, or another suitable material.

Additionally, nesting boxes or designated areas within the enclosure can be provided to mimic natural nesting sites. These areas should be designed to allow easy excavation by the female, as she will dig a hole to deposit her eggs. Proper temperature and humidity control within the nesting area are critical to the success of egg-laying.

The female should be provided with privacy and minimal disturbances during the egg-laying process. Stress or disruptions can potentially lead to egg retention or abandonment of the nest site. Therefore, it's essential to limit human interaction and closely monitor the female from a distance.

After the eggs are laid, they should be carefully collected and transferred to an incubation chamber, especially if the reptile species practices egg retention. Proper incubation conditions, including temperature and humidity, should be maintained to ensure the development of healthy hatchlings. If the female remains with the eggs, ensure that she continues to receive appropriate care, including access to food and water.

Monitoring gestation periods and preparing for egg-laying require a combination of attentive observation and providing the right environmental conditions. A deep understanding of the specific requirements of the reptile species is paramount to achieving successful egg-laying and hatchling development. Proper care during these critical stages contributes significantly to the overall success of a reptile breeding program and the conservation of vulnerable or endangered species.

Post-birth care for mother and hatchlings

Post-birth care is a crucial phase in the reptile breeding

process that involves providing essential care and support to both the mother and her hatchlings. This period encompasses various aspects of husbandry, ensuring the well-being of the adult female after laying eggs and the proper care of the vulnerable hatchlings during their early stages of life.

Care for the Mother

Once the female has laid her eggs and completed her reproductive duties, it's essential to provide her with the necessary care to ensure her recovery and continued health.

After egg-laying, many female reptiles may be dehydrated and exhausted. It's crucial to offer clean, fresh water and a well-balanced diet to help them regain their strength. Hydrating the female through misting or offering water dishes is particularly important, as egg production can be physically demanding.

To minimize stress and potential harm to the female, it's advisable to keep her isolated from other reptiles or disturbances during the post-birth period. Providing a quiet, undisturbed environment allows her to rest and recover.

Regularly monitor the female's health and behavior. Any signs of illness or complications should be promptly addressed by a veterinarian with expertise in reptile care. It's essential to ensure that she is free from any retained eggs, as this condition can be life-threatening.

Hatchling Care

The care of hatchlings is a critical aspect of post-birth care. Hatchlings are often vulnerable and require specific conditions and attention to ensure their survival and healthy development.

In many cases, hatchlings should be separated from the adult female and any potential predators or aggressive tank mates. Isolation in a separate enclosure or nursery tank ensures their safety and allows for easier monitoring.

Providing the correct temperature and humidity levels is vital for hatchling reptiles, as these conditions can significantly impact their health and development. Consult speciesspecific guidelines to ensure that the environment is appropriately maintained.

Choosing an appropriate substrate for the hatchlings is essential for their well-being. Substrates should be safe and provide a suitable texture for them to move on. Additionally, providing hiding spots or shelters allows hatchlings to feel secure and reduces stress.

Dietary requirements for hatchlings can vary greatly between species. Understanding their specific nutritional needs is crucial. Some reptiles are herbivorous, while others are carnivorous or insectivorous. Providing the appropriate prey items or plant matter is essential to their growth and development.

Minimize handling and interaction with hatchlings, as excessive stress can be detrimental to their health. If handling is necessary for health checks or other reasons, it should be done gently and infrequently. Allow them to acclimate to their environment and establish feeding patterns before any significant handling.

Regularly monitor the health and behavior of hatchlings. Pay attention to signs of illness, inadequate feeding, or stress. Early intervention in case of health issues is essential for hatchling survival.

Record Keeping

Maintaining detailed records of both the mother's post-birth care and the development of hatchlings is essential for tracking progress and making informed decisions regarding their care. Record important information such as birth dates, health observations, feeding schedules, and any changes in environmental conditions.

Gradual Transition

As hatchlings grow and mature, it may become necessary to transition them to larger enclosures or habitats that better suit their adult requirements. This process should be gradual, with close monitoring to ensure they adapt successfully to their new environment.

Post-birth care for mother and hatchlings is a multifaceted process that encompasses several crucial aspects of reptile breeding. Ensuring the mother's recovery and well-being, along with providing appropriate care for hatchlings, is essential for successful breeding outcomes and the conservation of reptile species. Attention to detail, speciesspecific knowledge, and a commitment to providing the necessary care and support are key to fostering the health and survival of both the adult female and her precious hatchlings.

Chapter 7

Enrichment and Mental Stimulation

Enrichment and mental stimulation are essential components of reptile care. They involve providing a stimulating and engaging environment for reptiles to prevent boredom and promote their mental well-being. Enrichment can include offering a variety of hiding spots, objects to explore, and puzzles to solve. It helps reptiles exhibit natural behaviors, reduces stress, and enhances their overall quality of life.

Importance of Mental Stimulation for Reptiles

The impact of mental health on overall wellbeing

It's essential to recognize that mental health, though distinct from human mental health, plays a vital role in the overall wellbeing of these creatures. While reptiles may not possess emotions or consciousness in the same way humans do, their mental well-being is reflected in their behavior and overall health.

One significant aspect of reptile mental health is environmental enrichment. Providing a stimulating and dynamic environment within their enclosures can have a positive impact. This includes offering a variety of hiding spots, objects to explore, and opportunities for physical activity. For example, providing branches or climbing structures for arboreal reptiles like chameleons or tree snakes allows them to exhibit their natural behaviors and promotes mental stimulation.

Another consideration is the provision of proper lighting and temperature gradients within the enclosure. Reptiles often rely on external environmental cues to regulate their biological processes, such as thermoregulation and daily activity patterns. Maintaining proper lighting and temperature conditions not only ensures their physical well-being but also contributes to their mental health by allowing them to exhibit natural behaviors and circadian rhythms.

Social interactions, to the extent that they apply to the specific species, can also influence reptile mental well-being. Several Species of reptiles are solitary, while others are social or semi-social. Understanding the social dynamics of the species in question and offering appropriate socialization opportunities or ensuring solitude, as required, can contribute to their mental health.

Stress reduction is paramount in reptile care. Stress can negatively affect their overall health and can manifest in various ways, such as decreased appetite, erratic behavior, or even illness. Reducing stressors in their environment, such as sudden loud noises, excessive handling, or overcrowding, is essential to maintaining their mental wellbeing.

Observing reptile behavior is a crucial aspect of assessing their mental health. Changes in behavior patterns, such as excessive hiding, aggression, or listlessness, can be indicative of stress or discomfort. Recognizing these signs and taking appropriate measures to address the underlying causes is essential.

Examples of cognitive abilities in different reptile species

Cognitive abilities among reptile species vary widely, reflecting their distinct adaptations and behaviors in different environments. While reptiles may not possess the advanced cognitive functions seen in mammals or birds, they display a range of behaviors that showcase their cognitive skills.

Tortoises, characterized by their slow pace, exhibit remarkable spatial memory. Many tortoise species can traverse large territories while remembering precise locations of essential resources like food and water. This spatial memory is vital for their survival, especially in arid habitats where resources are scarce.

Chameleons are known for their exceptional visual perception. Their independently mobile eyes and depth perception enable them to locate prey and predators with remarkable precision.

Chameleons can also change color and patterns for communication and camouflage, demonstrating their cognitive flexibility.

Monitor lizards display problem-solving abilities. In captive settings, they can manipulate objects to access food and have been observed opening simple latches or gates. This illustrates their capacity for learning and applying problem-solving strategies.

Crocodilians, including crocodiles and alligators, engage in cooperative hunting behaviors. They work together to trap and capture prey, showcasing a level of social cognition that requires communication and coordination among individuals.

Various turtle species have developed sophisticated foraging techniques. Some turtles, like the loggerhead sea turtle, use their front flippers to dislodge prey from the seafloor, demonstrating their ability to learn and adapt for efficient feeding.

Green iguanas are known for their ability to learn and adapt. They can recognize their human caregivers, associate them with food, and learn to approach them for treats, indicating a degree of associative learning and memory.

Tegus, a group of large lizards, have demonstrated problem-solving skills in captivity. They can navigate mazes and solve simple puzzles to access rewards, indicating cognitive flexibility and problem-solving ability.

Sea turtles exhibit remarkable navigational skills during long-distance migrations. They can accurately navigate across vast oceanic distances, returning to specific nesting sites after years at sea. Their navigation abilities likely rely on a combination of celestial cues, geomagnetic fields, and memory.

Caimans, a type of small crocodilian, exhibit cognitive abilities in nest building. Female caimans construct nests with specific temperature and humidity conditions to influence the sex ratio of their offspring, demonstrating a form of environmental cognition and parental investment.

Practical Applications of Environmental Enrichment

Environmental enrichment is a fundamental aspect of reptile care, enhancing their physical and mental well-being by simulating natural behaviors and providing stimulating environments. Practical applications of environmental enrichment are essential for promoting reptile health and ensuring their overall quality of life.

Enclosure Design:

One of the most practical applications of environmental

enrichment is the design and layout of the reptile enclosure. Enclosures should mimic the reptile's natural habitat as closely as possible, taking into consideration factors such as substrate, hiding spots, and climbing structures. For terrestrial reptiles, providing a variety of textures and substrate depths encourages digging and burrowing behaviors. Similarly, arboreal reptiles benefit from vertical space and the presence of branches or perches for climbing and basking.

Hiding Spots and Shelter:

Reptiles often require hiding spots or shelters to feel secure and reduce stress. These can be provided in the form of naturalistic hides or purpose-built structures. The availability of hiding spots allows reptiles to exhibit their natural behaviors, such as seeking refuge from perceived threats or regulating their body temperature.

Climbing and Basking Opportunities

Many reptiles are adapted for climbing or basking in the wild. Providing opportunities for these behaviors is crucial. Enclosures for arboreal reptiles should include branches, vines, or platforms to facilitate climbing, while terrestrial species benefit from elevated basking spots under heat sources.

Environmental Variability

Reptiles thrive in environments with variability. This can include changes in temperature, humidity, and lighting. Mimicking natural temperature gradients within the enclosure allows reptiles to thermoregulate, moving between warmer and cooler areas as needed. Additionally, providing different lighting conditions, such as day-night cycles, contributes to their circadian rhythms and overall well-being.

Foraging and Feeding Enrichment

Encouraging natural foraging and hunting behaviors is another practical application of environmental enrichment. Scatter-feeding or hiding food items within the enclosure prompts reptiles to search for their meals, stimulating both physical and mental activity. This approach mimics their wild feeding behaviors, promoting a healthier appetite and reducing boredom.

Sensory Stimulation

Reptiles rely on their senses for survival. Incorporating sensory stimulation into their environment can include introducing new scents, textures, or visual stimuli. Providing a variety of substrate types, such as sand, soil, or leaf litter, allows reptiles to explore different textures and scents, engaging their senses.

Behavioral Training and Enrichment Devices

In some cases, behavioral training and enrichment devices can be employed. These may include puzzle feeders, mazes, or toys that encourage cognitive engagement. Reptiles can learn to interact with these devices to obtain rewards, promoting mental stimulation.

Rotating Enrichment Items

To prevent habituation and maintain interest, it's advisable to rotate and vary enrichment items regularly. Reptiles can become accustomed to their surroundings, so introducing novelty in the form of new objects or rearranged furnishings keeps their environment engaging.

DIY Enrichment Ideas

Crafting puzzle feeders and foraging opportunities

Creating DIY enrichment items for reptiles can be a rewarding and cost-effective way to promote their physical and mental well-being. Puzzle feeders and foraging opportunities are excellent choices, as they encourage natural behaviors and stimulate cognitive engagement.

Puzzle feeders are designed to make mealtime more interactive for reptiles. They require the reptile to work for their food, mimicking the foraging and hunting behaviors they exhibit in the wild. One idea is to cut a cardboard egg carton into individual compartments and place food items, such as insects or small portions of fruits and vegetables, into each compartment. The reptile must explore and manipulate the carton to access the hidden treats. Another option is repurposing a clean plastic bottle with a screwon lid by cutting small openings in the bottle to allow food to dispense gradually. Fill the bottle with insects or other suitable prey items. As the reptile nudges or rolls the bottle, food will slowly emerge, requiring effort and engagement. Additionally, you can create a "hide and seek" feeder by placing food items within naturalistic hides or small containers within the enclosure, encouraging exploration and mental stimulation.

Foraging opportunities stimulate a reptile's natural curiosity and problem-solving abilities. These activities encourage reptiles to explore their surroundings and engage with their environment. You can create a burrowing box by filling a box with a suitable substrate like coconut coir or reptile-safe soil and burying food items or treats within the substrate. This encourages reptiles to dig and search for the hidden rewards. Another idea is leaf litter hunting, where you collect clean, dry leaves from non-toxic plants and scatter them within the enclosure. Hide small food items or insects beneath the leaves to encourage foraging and exploration. Additionally, you can make a bamboo tube puzzle by cutting a length of bamboo into sections, leaving one end sealed. Fill the open end with food items or treats and seal it with a plug or cork. The reptile must roll or manipulate the bamboo to access the rewards. Finally, an obstacle course can be created within the enclosure using reptile-safe materials. Include tunnels, ramps, and platforms, and place food items or prey at various points within the course. The reptile will need to navigate the obstacles to reach the rewards.

When implementing DIY enrichment ideas, it's essential to consider the safety and suitability of materials used. Ensure that all items are clean, non-toxic, and free from potential hazards. Additionally, monitor the reptile's interaction with these enrichment items to ensure they are not causing stress or frustration. DIY puzzle feeders and foraging opportunities not only provide mental stimulation but also offer a form of physical exercise. These activities are particularly beneficial for reptiles with high energy levels and intelligence, such as monitor lizards, iguanas, and certain snake species. Tailoring DIY enrichment to the specific needs and preferences of your reptile can enhance their overall quality of life in captivity while fostering their natural behaviors.

Building climbing structures and hiding spots

Creating climbing structures and hiding spots within a reptile's enclosure is a practical and effective way to enhance their habitat and promote their overall well-being. These elements provide reptiles with opportunities to engage in natural behaviors, reduce stress, and establish a more enriching environment.

Many reptiles are naturally adapted for climbing in their natural habitats, and replicating this behavior in captivity can be highly beneficial. Building climbing structures allows reptiles to exercise their muscles, explore different elevations, and bask under various lighting conditions.

When building climbing structures, it's essential to choose materials that are safe for reptiles and easy to clean. Natural branches or commercially available reptile-safe branches can be used to create climbing surfaces. Ensure that any fasteners or connectors are secure and do not pose a risk of injury.

Create climbing structures with varying heights and textures to offer a range of experiences for your reptile. Different species may prefer different types of surfaces, such as smooth branches, rough bark, or textured vines.

Ensure that climbing structures are securely anchored

to prevent accidental falls or collapses. Properly affix them to the enclosure's walls or substrate, considering the size and weight of the reptile.

Place branches strategically to allow for easy access to basking spots, hiding areas, and different levels of the enclosure. Reptiles should be able to move between branches comfortably.

Incorporate basking platforms or shelves within the climbing structure, providing reptiles with a place to thermoregulate under heat sources. Ensure that the platform is stable and provides an appropriate distance from the heat source.

Hiding spots are essential for reptiles, as they provide security and a refuge from potential stressors. These spots mimic natural hiding places, allowing reptiles to retreat when they feel threatened or need privacy.

Utilize natural materials like cork bark, rock formations, or hollow logs to create hiding spots that resemble the reptile's natural environment. These materials not only provide shelter but also contribute to the aesthetic appeal of the enclosure.

Offer multiple hiding spots of varying sizes and shapes to accommodate the needs of different reptiles and provide choices for exploration. Hides should be placed throughout the enclosure, ensuring accessibility regardless of the reptile's location.

Some reptiles are burrowers and benefit from hideaways that allow them to dig into a substrate. Consider incorporating hides with openings beneath the substrate's surface to cater to these species.

Ensure that the entrances to hiding spots are appropriately sized for the reptile, preventing them from getting stuck or feeling trapped. Reptiles should be able to enter and exit their hiding spots comfortably.

Hides should offer a sense of privacy and security, with interiors that are not overly exposed. This allows reptiles to retreat to a concealed area when needed, reducing stress and promoting natural behaviors.

By incorporating climbing structures and hiding spots into a reptile's enclosure, caregivers create a more enriching and natural environment. These additions encourage physical activity, mental stimulation, and the expression of instinctual behaviors. Moreover, they contribute to the overall well-being and contentment of the reptile, helping them thrive in captivity.

Incorporating natural elements for sensory stimulation

Incorporating natural elements into a reptile's enclosure is a valuable strategy for providing sensory stimulation and enhancing their overall well-being. These elements engage the reptile's senses and create a more immersive and enriching environment that closely resembles their natural habitat.

Substrate Selection

Choosing an appropriate substrate is a crucial step in

replicating a reptile's natural environment. Different species have specific substrate preferences based on their natural habitat. For instance, desert-dwelling reptiles may thrive on a sandy substrate, while forest dwellers may require leaf litter or moss. The substrate not only provides a comfortable surface for the reptile but also engages their sense of touch as they interact with it.

Natural Scents

Reptiles rely on their sense of smell to detect food, recognize mates, and navigate their surroundings. Introducing natural scents from the reptile's native environment can be a stimulating experience. This can be achieved by incorporating items like leaves, branches, or rocks from the reptile's natural habitat. The scent of these materials can evoke a sense of familiarity and curiosity in the reptile, encouraging exploration.

Texture Variety

Offering a variety of textures within the enclosure engages the reptile's sense of touch. This can include providing rough surfaces like rocks or branches for climbing and basking, as well as soft substrates for burrowing or lounging. Textural diversity allows the reptile to experience different sensations as they move and interact with their environment.

Natural Decor

Utilizing natural decor items such as driftwood, rocks, or plant materials not only adds aesthetic value but also provides sensory stimulation. Reptiles may use these items for climbing, perching, or rubbing against, engaging both their tactile and proprioceptive senses.

Auditory Stimulation:

While reptiles are not known for their acute hearing, they can still perceive vibrations and low-frequency sounds. Incorporating elements like flowing water, gentle rustling leaves, or ambient sounds can provide subtle auditory stimulation. However, it's essential to ensure that any auditory elements do not cause stress or discomfort to the reptile.

Visual Enrichment

Reptiles also rely on their vision to interpret their environment. Mimicking natural lighting conditions with appropriate UVB and heat sources is essential. Additionally, adding live plants or artificial foliage can create hiding spots, visual barriers, and opportunities for the reptile to explore and visually interact with their enclosure.

Temperature Gradients:

Temperature gradients within the enclosure are not only important for thermoregulation but also engage the reptile's sense of touch. By providing various temperature zones, including warmer basking spots and cooler resting areas, reptiles can choose the sensation they prefer at any given time.

Incorporating natural elements for sensory stimulation contributes to a more holistic and enriching captive environment for reptiles. These elements engage multiple senses, encouraging exploration, foraging, and the expression of natural behaviors. When selecting and arranging natural elements, it's crucial to consider the specific needs and preferences of the reptile species to ensure that the sensory experience is both enriching and comfortable.

Creating a Stimulating Environment

Implementing a rotational schedule for enrichment items

Maintaining a stimulating environment is essential for the well-being of captive reptiles. One effective approach to achieve this is by implementing a rotational schedule for enrichment items. This strategy ensures that the reptile's enclosure remains dynamic and engaging over time, preventing boredom and promoting natural behaviors.

A rotational enrichment schedule involves periodically introducing new items, toys, or features into the reptile's enclosure while removing or rearranging existing ones. This process prevents habituation, where the reptile becomes overly accustomed to its surroundings and potentially loses interest in its environment. By regularly changing elements within the enclosure, caregivers can encourage exploration and interaction.

The introduction of novel items or changes in the enclosure's layout stimulates the reptile's curiosity. Reptiles are naturally inclined to explore their surroundings, and novel objects or rearrangements provide them with opportunities for discovery. This not only engages their cognitive faculties but also promotes physical activity.

Enrichment items can vary widely and include objects like puzzle feeders, hideaways, climbing structures, and even visual or auditory stimuli. These items cater to the reptile's natural behaviors, such as foraging, hiding, climbing, or exploring. For example, a puzzle feeder with hidden food items encourages the reptile to search for its meals, mimicking hunting behavior.

Implementing a rotational schedule allows caregivers to simulate environmental variation. In the wild, reptiles experience changes in their habitat due to seasonal shifts, weather patterns, and resource availability. By periodically altering the enclosure, caregivers replicate this natural variability, which can positively impact the reptile's mental and physical health.

Reptiles are not immune to boredom, and long periods of inactivity or monotony can lead to stress or behavioral issues. Rotational enrichment keeps the reptile mentally engaged and prevents them from becoming lethargic or disinterested. Boredom reduction is especially important for highly intelligent species, such as monitor lizards or iguanas.

While implementing a rotational schedule, it's essential to monitor the reptile's responses and preferences. Not all reptiles will react the same way to enrichment items, so caregivers should adapt their approach based on individual reactions. Some reptiles may take a keen interest in new items, while others may require time to acclimate.

When introducing new items, safety is paramount. Ensure that any enrichment items are non-toxic, free from potential hazards, and appropriate for the reptile's size and species. Regularly inspect and clean items to maintain a hygienic environment.

Creating an enrichment calendar can help caregivers plan and schedule rotational changes effectively. This calendar can outline when to introduce new items, when to rearrange the enclosure, and when to remove or replace worn-out items. Consistency in the enrichment schedule ensures that the reptile continually experiences a stimulating environment.

Using Seasonal Changes to Stimulate Natural Behaviors:

Recreating seasonal changes within a captive reptile's enclosure is a powerful method to stimulate natural behaviors and enhance their overall well-being. By mimicking the environmental fluctuations that reptiles experience in the wild, caregivers can encourage physical activity, breeding behaviors, and foraging instincts. Here's a detailed exploration of how seasonal changes can be utilized to promote these natural behaviors:

In many reptile species, seasonal variations in temperature and light play a pivotal role in regulating metabolic activity and behavior. By adjusting the enclosure's temperature and lighting to mimic seasonal changes, caregivers can influence the reptile's activity levels, feeding habits, and reproductive behaviors. For instance, providing cooler temperatures and shorter daylight hours can simulate a winter-like period, inducing a slowdown in metabolism and potentially encouraging hibernation-like behaviors in some species.

Seasonal cues are critical for triggering reproductive behaviors in many reptiles. The transition from a cooler, winter-like period to a warmer, spring-like period can signal to reptiles that it's time to mate. Caregivers can replicate these seasonal changes by gradually increasing temperatures and daylight hours within the enclosure. This can stimulate courtship rituals, mating, and egg-laying behaviors in species that rely on seasonal cues for reproduction.

In the wild, reptiles often exhibit increased activity during warmer seasons when prey is more abundant. By adjusting the enclosure's temperature and lighting to simulate the onset of spring and summer, caregivers can encourage higher activity levels. This, in turn, promotes natural foraging behaviors, as reptiles become more active in search of food.

Seasonal changes in the availability of prey and vegetation can impact a reptile's diet. Caregivers can adjust the reptile's diet to reflect these seasonal shifts. For example, during the warmer months, when prey is more plentiful, caregivers can offer a greater variety of live insects or fresh vegetation. During colder months, when food may be scarcer, a reduced feeding schedule can mimic natural fasting periods.

Simulating seasonal changes can be an excellent form of environmental enrichment. Introducing seasonal decorations or altering the enclosure's layout to reflect the changing seasons can pique the reptile's curiosity and encourage exploration. For example, incorporating fallen leaves, seasonal flowers, or changing the substrate to mimic a seasonal shift can engage the reptile's senses and provide mental stimulation.

Caregivers should closely monitor the reptile's response to seasonal changes and make adjustments as needed. Not all reptiles will react the same way to simulated seasons, and individual preferences can vary. Caregivers should adapt the environmental changes based on the reptile's behavior, ensuring that it remains comfortable and healthy throughout the seasonal transitions.

While recreating seasonal changes, caregivers must prioritize the reptile's safety and comfort. Ensure that temperature and humidity levels remain within the species' acceptable range, preventing extremes that could stress or harm the reptile. Regularly monitor environmental conditions and make necessary adjustments to maintain the reptile's well-being.

The Role of Human Interaction in Mental Stimulation for Reptiles:

Human interaction can play a significant role in providing mental stimulation for captive reptiles. While reptiles are not typically social animals, and their interactions differ from those of mammals or birds, they can still benefit from positive and non-invasive interactions with their caregivers. Here's a detailed exploration of the role of human interaction in mental stimulation for reptiles:

Observation and Engagement

Human caregivers can observe their reptiles' behavior, which provides an opportunity to learn about the reptile's preferences, habits, and overall well-being. This observation can help caregivers identify changes in behavior that may indicate stress, illness, or other issues. Additionally, caregivers can engage with their reptiles through careful and non-invasive means, such as quietly sitting near the enclosure and allowing the reptile to become accustomed to their presence.

Handling and Taming

Some reptiles can be tamed to tolerate gentle handling. While not all reptile species are comfortable with handling, those that are can benefit from short, stress-free handling sessions. Taming reptiles can make health checks, veterinary visits, and enclosure maintenance less stressful for both the caregiver and the reptile. It is essential to research the specific handling requirements and preferences of the reptile species in question and avoid overhandling, which can lead to stress.

Positive Enrichment

Human interaction can be incorporated into enrichment activities. For example, caregivers can use hand-feeding as a form of positive reinforcement training, where the reptile associates the caregiver's presence with food rewards. This not only stimulates the reptile mentally but also strengthens the bond between the reptile and caregiver. It's crucial to use appropriate and species-specific food items for hand-feeding and to avoid overfeeding or disrupting the reptile's regular feeding schedule.

Environmental Changes

Human interaction can also facilitate environmental changes within the enclosure. Caregivers can rearrange the enclosure, introduce new hiding spots, or offer novel items that encourage exploration and mental engagement. For example, moving decor items or providing new climbing structures can pique the reptile's curiosity and stimulate their interest.

Preventing Stress

Caregivers must approach interactions with sensitivity to the reptile's stress levels. Overhandling, sudden and loud movements, or disturbing the reptile during its rest or basking periods can lead to stress and negatively impact the reptile's mental wellbeing. Understanding the reptile's natural behaviors and preferences is essential for creating positive interactions.

Bond and Trust

While reptiles may not form social bonds in the same way mammals do, they can develop a sense of trust and familiarity with their caregivers over time. Consistent, non-threatening interactions can help build this trust, making the reptile more comfortable with the caregiver's presence and reducing stress.

Respect for Individual Differences

It's essential to recognize that individual reptiles within the same species can have varying temperaments and preferences. Some reptiles may be more receptive to human interaction, while others may prefer minimal disturbance. Caregivers should always respect the individual needs and boundaries of their reptiles.

Chapter 8

Reptile Species Profiles

Reptile species profiles provide concise information about different reptile species, including their habitat, behavior, dietary preferences, and care requirements. These profiles serve as valuable references for caregivers, helping them understand and meet the specific needs of each reptile species they keep.

In-depth Care Guides for Popular Reptile Species

Bearded Dragons

Bearded dragons, scientifically known as Pogona vitticeps, are one of the most beloved reptile pets due to their captivating appearance and generally docile nature.

Ensuring their well-being begins with creating a suitable habitat that closely resembles their natural environment. Adequate enclosure size is essential; for a single adult bearded dragon, a 40-gallon tank is the minimum, though larger enclosures are preferable. Tanks of 75 gallons or more offer ample space for these reptiles to move and explore.

Choosing an appropriate substrate is critical. Options

like reptile carpet, paper towels, or a mixture of organic soil and play sand are safe choices. It's important to avoid substrates that can be ingested, such as loose sand, as this can lead to impaction.

Bearded dragons require UVB lighting for proper calcium absorption. Full-spectrum UVB bulbs should be installed above the basking area, along with a basking bulb to create the necessary temperature gradient. Maintaining a basking spot temperature between 95-105°F (35-40°C) and a cooler side ranging from 75-85°F (24-29°C) ensures the reptile can thermoregulate effectively. Nighttime temperatures can slightly drop, but extreme cold should be avoided.

In terms of humidity, bearded dragons thrive in low humidity environments, typically around 30-40%. Adequate ventilation within the enclosure helps maintain the right humidity levels. To provide a balanced diet, remember that bearded dragons are omnivorous, enjoying a mix of live insects, vegetables, and occasional fruits. Live insects such as crickets, dubia roaches, and mealworms should be offered, with appropriate dusting of calcium and vitamin D3 supplements.

Their vegetable intake should include dark, leafy greens like collard greens, kale, and mustard greens, along with vegetables such as bell peppers and squash. Occasional fruits, like berries, can be included. It's crucial to provide variety to ensure a balanced diet.

Bearded dragons obtain most of their hydration from food, but a shallow water dish should still be available with clean water that is regularly changed. Feeding schedules can vary depending on age; juvenile dragons may require daily feedings, while adults can be fed every other day. Monitoring their weight and overall health helps determine the appropriate feeding schedule.

Health concerns for bearded dragons include metabolic bone disease (MBD), respiratory infections, and parasites. Proper lighting, diet, and hygiene are critical in preventing these conditions. Regular veterinary check-ups are recommended to ensure the reptile's health and to address any potential issues promptly.

Bearded dragons are known for their generally docile nature, making them a favorite choice for reptile enthusiasts. Individual temperaments can vary, but most bearded dragons can become accustomed to handling and interaction with their caregivers. Building trust through gentle handling and understanding their unique behavioral traits, such as head-bobbing or arm-waving, ensures a happy and healthy life for these captivating reptiles.

Ball Pythons

Ball pythons (Python regius) are one of the most popular snake species kept as pets due to their manageable size and calm demeanor. Proper care is essential to ensure their well-being throughout their lives. The following information will include details on enclosure setup, feeding and temperature requirements at different life stages, and common behavioral patterns and handling tips for ball pythons.

Setting up an appropriate enclosure is crucial for ball pythons. The enclosure size should be based on the snake's age and size. A young ball python can thrive in a 20-30-gallon terrarium, while adult snakes require a 40-50gallon tank. Enclosures should have a secure lid to prevent escapes.

Choosing the right substrate is essential. Options like aspen shavings, cypress mulch, or coconut husk bedding are suitable. Providing multiple hiding spots using reptile caves or half logs is important. Ball pythons appreciate a hide on both the warm and cool sides of their enclosure to feel secure.

Feeding ball pythons depends on their age and size. Young snakes typically feed on small rodents, while adults consume larger ones. Feed your snake appropriate-sized prey, ensuring it is roughly the same width as the snake's widest part. Prey items should be thawed and warmed to the snake's preferred temperature before feeding.

Maintaining the right temperature gradient is crucial. Provide a basking spot with a temperature of around 88-92°F

(31-33°C) and a cooler side ranging from 75-80°F (24-27°C).

Nighttime temperatures can slightly drop, but make sure it remains within an acceptable range. Use under-tank heating pads or ceramic heat emitters to create these temperature zones.

Ball pythons are known for their gentle disposition, but they can be shy and may take time to acclimate to handling. When handling a ball python, approach slowly and confidently. Start with short sessions, gradually increasing the duration as the snake becomes more comfortable.

Ball pythons often ball up into a tight coil when they feel threatened or stressed, which is how they got their name. It's a natural defense mechanism. Allow your snake to relax and explore at its own pace. Handling should be done gently, supporting the snake's body properly.

Regular handling helps tame ball pythons, making them more accustomed to human interaction. However, they may prefer to rest in their hiding spots, especially during daylight hours, as they are nocturnal.

Leopard Geckos

Leopard geckos (Eublepharis macularius) are popular reptile pets known for their striking appearance and relatively straightforward care requirements. Now we will dive into details on terrarium setup, specialized dietary needs and supplementation requirements, as well as breeding considerations, including incubation and neonatal care for leopard geckos.

Creating the ideal terrarium for leopard geckos is essential to provide them with a comfortable and stimulating environment. Enclosures should be escape-proof, with a secure lid or top. The size of the enclosure depends on the number of geckos and their age.

For substrate, options like paper towels, reptile carpet, or a mixture of calcium sand and organic topsoil can be used. Ensure that the substrate is not ingested during feeding, as impaction can occur.

Leopard geckos appreciate a variety of hiding spots and decor elements. Provide at least one hide on the warm and cool sides of the enclosure, along with branches or flat rocks for climbing and basking. Ensure that there are no sharp edges or potentially hazardous objects in the enclosure.

Leopard geckos have specific dietary requirements that need to be met for their wellbeing. They are insectivorous, primarily consuming live insects. Common feeder insects include crickets, mealworms, dubia roaches, and waxworms. Variety in their diet is essential to ensure they receive a balanced nutrition profile.

Supplementation is vital to provide essential vitamins and minerals. Dust feeder insects with calcium powder containing vitamin D3 two to three times a week for adult geckos and more frequently for juveniles.

Multivitamin supplements can be used once a week to ensure they receive all necessary nutrients.

Always provide a shallow dish of clean, dechlorinated

water in the enclosure. While leopard geckos do not typically drink large amounts of water, it's essential to maintain hydration.

Breeding leopard geckos can be a rewarding but intricate process. A male and female leopard gecko should be paired during the breeding season, typically in the spring. Successful mating can result in egg production.

The female leopard gecko will lay a clutch of eggs, which should be carefully collected and placed in an incubator set at around 82-88°F (28-31°C). Proper humidity levels in the incubator are crucial, typically around 70-80%.

Incubation time varies but usually takes about 40-70 days. Monitor the eggs for signs of fertility and ensure proper ventilation during incubation.

After hatching, neonatal care involves providing small enclosures with appropriate substrate, temperature, and humidity levels. Hatchlings should be fed with appropriately sized insects and monitored for proper growth and health.

Reticulated Pythons

Reticulated pythons (Python reticulatus) are among the largest snake species globally, known for their impressive size and striking pattern. Providing proper care for these magnificent reptiles is crucial to ensure their health and well-being.

Reticulated pythons are among the largest snakes in the world and can grow to substantial lengths, making their enclosure needs quite specific. Due to their size and activity level, a custom-built enclosure is often necessary for adult reticulated pythons. The enclosure should be spacious and escape-proof, with secure locks and a sturdy lid.

For a juvenile reticulated python, a large enclosure with a minimum length of 4-6 feet is suitable. As they grow, larger enclosures will be required. Adult reticulated pythons may need enclosures measuring 8-12 feet or more in length. Provide a basking area with a temperature gradient, hiding spots, and climbing opportunities.

Reticulated pythons are carnivorous and have a broad diet in the wild, consuming birds, mammals, and occasionally even other reptiles. In captivity, their diet primarily consists of appropriately sized rodents. The size of the prey should be in proportion to the snake's girth, ensuring that it does not present a choking hazard. Hatchlings can start with small mice, progressing to larger rats as they grow.

Feeding frequency varies with age and size. Juveniles may require weekly feedings, while adults can be fed every 2-4 weeks. Always feed pre-killed or pre-frozen prey items to ensure the snake's safety.

Handling reticulated pythons should be done with caution and only by experienced handlers due to their size and strength. When handling, support the snake's body properly, and be aware of their temperament. These snakes can be unpredictable and may become stressed or defensive, especially if they feel threatened. It's essential to pay close attention to their body language.

Signs of stress or health issues in reticulated pythons include:

- Frequent hissing or striking.
- Defensive postures, such as coiling up and raising the head.
- Refusal to eat.
- Weight loss.
- Abnormal shedding or retained shed skin.
- Respiratory issues, such as wheezing or excessive mouth breathing.
- Prolonged periods of inactivity or hiding.

If any of these signs are observed, it's crucial to consult a veterinarian experienced in reptile care. Regular veterinary check-ups are also recommended to ensure the snake's health.

Burmese Pythons

Burmese pythons (Python bivittatus) are large and powerful constrictor snakes native to Southeast Asia. Proper care is essential to ensure their well-being in captivity.

Creating the right habitat for Burmese pythons is crucial for their health and comfort. These snakes thrive in environments that mimic their natural habitat. A large and secure enclosure is necessary, as they can grow to impressive lengths. An enclosure measuring at least 8-10 feet in length is recommended for adult Burmese pythons.

Maintaining proper humidity levels is vital. Burmese pythons require a humidity range of 50-70%. This can be achieved by providing a large water dish, regular misting, and using appropriate substrates that retain moisture, such as cypress mulch or coconut coir.

Temperature gradients are essential for these snakes. Provide a basking spot with a temperature of 88-92°F (31-33°C) and a cooler side ranging from 75-85°F (24-29°C). Nighttime temperatures can drop slightly, but avoid extreme cold.

Burmese pythons are carnivorous and primarily consume appropriately sized mammals in captivity. Prey items should be in proportion to the snake's size and age. Hatchlings can start with small rodents, such as pinkie mice, and progress to larger prey items as they grow. Adult Burmese pythons can consume larger rodents, rabbits, or poultry.

Feeding frequency varies with age. Hatchlings and juveniles may require weekly or bi-weekly feedings, while adults can be fed every 2-4 weeks. Always feed pre-killed or pre-frozen prey to ensure the snake's safety.

Potential health issues to be aware of include obesity, regurgitation, and respiratory infections. Monitoring the snake's weight and eating habits can help prevent these issues. Regular veterinary check-ups are recommended to ensure their health.

Burmese pythons are known for their generally calm and docile temperament, which makes them appealing to reptile enthusiasts. However, it's essential to approach handling with care, especially for larger individuals. Always handle Burmese pythons gently and support their body correctly.

These snakes are generally tolerant of being handled but may become stressed if mishandled or if they feel threatened. Signs of stress can include hissing, defensive postures, or even attempting to strike. It's crucial to observe their body language and be respectful of their boundaries.

Colubrid Snakes

Colubrid snakes constitute a vast and diverse group within the world of reptiles, encompassing approximately two-thirds of all known snake species. These snakes are characterized by their non-venomous nature, setting them apart from other snake families that may possess venomous capabilities. Colubrids are distributed across almost every continent, with the exception of Antarctica, and display a wide range of care requirements, behaviors, and adaptations. It's important to recognize that colubrid snakes include numerous subfamilies and species, such as garter snakes, corn snakes, and rat snakes, among many others. Each of these colubrids may have unique care needs, dietary preferences, and habitat requirements, making it essential for reptile enthusiasts to research and understand the specific characteristics of the colubrid species they are keeping as pets. Proper care and attention to their individual needs are crucial for ensuring the health, wellbeing, and longevity of these fascinating and diverse reptiles.

Recognizing colubrid snakes can be challenging due to the diversity within this family, but there are some general characteristics and features that can help identify them.

Colubrids typically have slender heads that are not distinctly different from the rest of their body. They lack the wide, triangular heads associated with venomous snakes. Their bodies are usually long and slender with smooth scales, and their eyes are positioned on the sides of their heads, allowing for a broad field of vision.

Like all snakes, colubrids have a forked tongue they use for scent detection, but this feature is not exclusive to them. Their coloration varies widely, ranging from brightly colored to more subdued patterns, often even within the same species. Their belly scales are typically uniform and smooth.

In terms of behavior, colubrids are generally non-aggressive and non-venomous. They may hiss or strike if they feel threatened, but these are defensive behaviors and not indicative of venomous capabilities. They are primarily carnivorous, with a diet that includes insects, rodents, amphibians, and other small vertebrates. However, dietary preferences can vary among species.

Colubrid snakes inhabit various environments, such as forests, grasslands, and wetlands, with specific habitat preferences varying by species. They can be found on nearly every continent except Antarctica, and their geographic location can be a valuable clue in identifying a specific colubrid species.

While these characteristics can be helpful in identifying colubrid snakes, accurate identification may still be challenging, especially for individuals without extensive herpetological experience. When precise species recognition is essential, consulting with a reptile expert, herpetologist, or veterinarian with expertise in reptiles is recommended to ensure proper identification and care.

Colubrids encompass a wide variety of snake species, each with unique care requirements. Some common colubrid species include corn snakes, king snakes, and rat snakes. While care specifics can vary, there are some general guidelines that apply to many colubrids.

Enclosure size and design can vary depending on the species and size of the colubrid snake. A 20-30-gallon tank is suitable for most smaller species, while larger species may require larger enclosures. Ensure the enclosure has a secure lid or top to prevent escapes.

For substrate, options like aspen shavings, cypress mulch, or coconut coir are commonly used. Choose a substrate that holds humidity well but is also easy to clean. Provide hiding spots, branches, and climbing opportunities to accommodate the snake's natural behaviors.

Colubrids typically have carnivorous diets, primarily consisting of rodents, birds, and amphibians. Prey size should be appropriate for the snake's size, with hatchlings consuming smaller prey and larger individuals consuming larger prey items.

Feeding frequency varies with age and size. Hatchlings may require more frequent meals, while adults can be fed every 1-2 weeks. Always feed pre-killed or pre-frozen prey items.

Shedding is a natural process for all snakes, including colubrids. Proper humidity levels in the enclosure are essential to ensure successful shedding. A retained shed can lead to health issues, so monitor your snake during the shedding process and provide a shedding box or humid hide. If the snake seems to have 'stuck shed,' a soaking in room-temperature water might help release the shed. Ensuring that shedding occurs without complications is crucial for the overall health and well-being of your colubrid snake.

Common health concerns for colubrids include respiratory infections, mites, and obesity. Proper hygiene, maintaining appropriate temperatures and humidity levels, and providing a balanced diet can help prevent these issues. Regular veterinary check-ups are recommended to ensure the snake's health.

Rankin's Dragons

Rankin's dragons (Pogona rankini), also known as Rankin's rock dragons or Kimberley rock monitors, are small and docile reptiles native to northern Australia. They are closely related to bearded dragons and share many care similarities. Following information contains details on the terrarium setup for Rankin's dragons, including lighting and heating specifics, their dietary needs, feeding schedules, and potential health issues, as well as their social behaviors and handling recommendations.

Creating a suitable terrarium for Rankin's dragons is essential to ensure their well-being. A 20-30-gallon tank is appropriate for a single adult dragon, though larger enclosures are better if space allows. These lizards are primarily terrestrial but also appreciate some climbing opportunities and hiding spots.

Provide a substrate such as reptile carpet, newspaper, or a mixture of organic topsoil and play sand. A shallow water dish should always be available, although Rankin's dragons obtain most of their hydration from their food.

Rankin's dragons, like many reptiles, require access to

UVB lighting to metabolize calcium properly. Full-spectrum UVB bulbs should be used and placed above the basking area. A basking bulb or ceramic heat emitter can provide the necessary temperature gradient, with a basking spot reaching around 95-105°F (35-40°C) and a cooler side between 75-85°F (24-29°C). Nighttime temperatures can drop slightly, but extreme cold should be avoided.

Rankin's dragons are omnivorous and enjoy a varied diet. Their primary food sources include insects, such as crickets, mealworms, and dubia roaches. Offer a variety of greens and vegetables, such as collard greens, kale, and carrots. Occasional fruit, like berries, can also be provided.

Feeding schedules can vary depending on the age of the dragon. Juveniles may require daily feedings, while adults can be fed every other day. Dusting insects with calcium and vitamin D3 supplements is essential for their health.

Common health issues for Rankin's dragons include metabolic bone disease (MBD), respiratory infections, and parasites. Providing proper UVB lighting, a balanced diet, and maintaining hygiene in the enclosure can help prevent these issues. Regular veterinary checkups are recommended to ensure their health.

Rankin's dragons are generally docile and can be socialized with regular handling. When handling, support their body properly, and be gentle to avoid stressing them. Like many reptiles, they may exhibit defensive behaviors if they feel threatened. Monitor their body language and allow them to become accustomed to handling gradually.

Crested Geckos

Crested geckos (Correlophus ciliatus) are fascinating and popular reptile pets known for their unique appearance and relatively easy care requirements. These geckos typically grow to a size of 7 to 9 inches (18 to 23 centimeters) in length.

Crested geckos are arboreal, meaning they spend most of their time in trees and on branches. Therefore, their enclosure should emphasize vertical space and provide ample opportunities for climbing and exploration. A tall terrarium or vivarium is ideal, with a minimum height of 18 inches for a single adult crested gecko.

Substrate options include coconut coir, cypress mulch, or a bioactive substrate mixture. Ensure that the substrate retains moisture well but does not become overly soggy. Crested geckos require high humidity levels, typically around 60-80%, which can be achieved through regular misting.

Provide multiple hiding spots and vertical branches or bamboo shoots for climbing. Artificial plants or live plants, such as pothos or ficus, can add to the enclosure's aesthetics and provide hiding spots.

Crested geckos are omnivorous and primarily consume fruit, nectar, and insects in the wild. In captivity, their diet mainly consists of commercially available crested gecko diet powder, which can be mixed with water to form a paste. Feed this prepared diet every other day, and ensure that it is age-appropriate, as younger geckos may require a different formula than adults.

Supplementation is essential to ensure proper nutrition. Dust the crested gecko diet with calcium and vitamin D3 supplements every other feeding. Multivitamin supplements can be used once a week.

Crested geckos are generally docile and can be handled, but they may become stressed if mishandled or if they feel threatened. When handling, approach them gently and support their body correctly. Allow them to walk onto your hand rather than grabbing or scooping them up.

Signs of stress in crested geckos may include hiding excessively, losing their tail (a natural defense mechanism), changes in coloration, and vocalizations (a soft chirping sound). If you notice any of these signs or suspect illness, consult a reptile veterinarian experienced in crested gecko care.

Regularly monitor your crested gecko for proper weight, as rapid weight loss can be a sign of underlying health issues.

Skinks

Skinks, members of the family Scincidae, encompass a diverse group of lizards known for their unique body shape and behavior. Caring for skinks in captivity requires careful attention to their specific habitat and dietary needs. One of the critical aspects of skink care is the enclosure design. Skinks typically require higher humidity levels compared to many other reptiles. The specific humidity requirements can vary depending on the skink species, but maintaining a humidity range of 50-80% is often recommended. Achieving this level of humidity can be done through regular misting of the enclosure, providing a water dish for drinking and soaking, and selecting a moisture-retaining substrate.

Substrate selection is another important consideration. Skinks appreciate substrates that can hold moisture effectively. Popular choices include coconut coir, cypress mulch, or a combination of peat moss and sand. The substrate should be deep enough to allow for burrowing, as many skink species are known to burrow for shelter and security.

Hiding places are essential for skinks due to their secretive nature. These lizards feel more secure when they have hiding spots to retreat to when they feel threatened or stressed.

Providing ample hiding spots within the enclosure, such as pieces of cork bark, driftwood, or artificial caves, can help reduce stress and promote a sense of security for skinks.

In addition to hiding places, some skink species are arboreal or semi-arboreal and benefit from climbing opportunities. This can be achieved by adding branches, vines, or other climbing structures to the enclosure, allowing skinks to engage in natural behaviors such as exploring and perching.

Temperature gradient is another vital aspect of enclosure design. Skinks require a temperature gradient within their enclosure, with a basking spot at one end reaching around 85-90°F (29-32°C) and a cooler side at the opposite end around 75-80°F (24-27°C). This gradient allows skinks to thermoregulate by moving between warmer and cooler areas as needed. Heat lamps or heat mats can be used to create and maintain these temperature zones.

Skink species have varied dietary preferences. Some are omnivorous, while others are primarily herbivorous or insectivorous. It's crucial to research and understand the specific dietary needs of your skink species to provide an appropriate diet. Feeding schedules can also vary, with juveniles often requiring more frequent feedings than adults. A diet that includes a variety of food items such as insects, fruits, vegetables, and specialized reptile diets (if required) is typically recommended.

As with all reptile pets, skinks can be susceptible to various health issues. Common concerns include respiratory infections, parasitic infestations, metabolic bone disease (MBD), and skin problems. To prevent these issues, maintain proper hygiene within the enclosure, provide appropriate humidity and temperature levels, and ensure a balanced diet.

Regular veterinary check-ups are advisable to monitor the health of your skink and address any potential health issues promptly.

Finally, when it comes to handling skinks, it's essential to be mindful of their shy and sometimes stressed nature. Many skinks may not tolerate frequent handling well and can become stressed or may drop their tails as a defense mechanism. If handling is necessary, it should be done gently and infrequently, allowing the skink to become accustomed to human interaction gradually. Providing hiding spots within the enclosure can also help skinks feel secure and reduce stress. Monitoring their behavior and appearance for signs of stress or illness is crucial for maintaining their overall well-being and ensuring they thrive in captivity.

Tortoises

Tortoises, known for their distinctive characteristics and impressive lifespans, require meticulous care that encompasses their habitat, dietary needs, and natural behaviors. Carefully considering both outdoor and indoor enclosure setups, understanding their dietary requirements and feeding schedules, acknowledging the need for hibernation in certain species, and recognizing and addressing their natural behaviors are all essential aspects of caring for tortoises.

Outdoor enclosures, often referred to as tortoise pens, are suitable for regions with favorable climates. These enclosures must prioritize safety, with secure fencing extending underground to deter digging predators. Access to natural sunlight is crucial, necessitating areas with both shade and direct sunlight. Additionally, a sheltered spot should be provided for the tortoise to escape adverse weather conditions. The enclosure should offer opportunities for natural foraging by planting tortoise-safe vegetation.

In regions with extreme climates or for species less adaptable to outdoor conditions, indoor enclosures become essential. These indoor spaces should be sufficiently spacious, allowing the tortoise room to move around, explore, and access hiding spots. Choosing an appropriate substrate, such as coconut coir or cypress mulch, helps recreate their natural habitat. Maintaining the correct temperature gradients is vital, with basking spots reaching 90-95°F (32-35°C) and a cooler side at 70-75°F (21-24°C). Full-spectrum UVB lighting is necessary to support their overall health.

Tortoises are herbivores, but their specific dietary needs

may vary by species. They should have access to fresh, clean water, as proper hydration is crucial for their health and well-being. Their diet should consist of leafy greens like kale, collard greens, and dandelion greens, along with high-fiber grass hays such as Timothy or Bermuda grass hay. Additionally, vegetables like carrots, squash, and bell peppers can be included, although fruits should be offered sparingly due to their high sugar content.

Calcium supplements should be used to prevent metabolic bone disease. Feeding schedules typically involve daily meals, with portion sizes tailored to the tortoise's size and age.

For some tortoise species, hibernation is a natural behavior. If you live in an area where hibernation is necessary, it's crucial to research the specific hibernation requirements of your tortoise species. Typically, this process involves reducing food intake, lowering temperatures, and providing a suitable hibernation chamber.

Recognizing and facilitating natural behaviors is essential for tortoise well-being. These reptiles engage in activities such as digging, basking, and exploring. To encourage these behaviors, provide hiding spots, digging areas, and access to a basking spot with appropriate temperatures and lighting. Creating an environment that mimics their natural habitat and closely observing their behavior allows you to better understand and meet their specific needs.

Chameleons

Chameleons, known for their remarkable ability to change colors and their independently moving eyes, require meticulous care to thrive in captivity. Essential aspects of their care include creating an appropriate enclosure, meeting their dietary requirements, handling them with care, and monitoring their well-being closely.

Enclosure design is a critical factor in chameleon care. These arboreal reptiles need vertical space more than horizontal, as they spend their lives climbing trees and shrubs. Taller enclosures with live plants and branches mimic their natural habitat, providing mental stimulation and exercise. Full-spectrum UVB lighting is essential for their calcium metabolism and overall health, so ensuring the correct lighting source is crucial. Maintaining proper humidity levels, typically around 5070%, is vital, achieved through regular misting and the presence of live plants.

Chameleons are insectivores, and their diet primarily consists of insects. The specific insects and feeding frequency can vary by species. Proper supplementation with calcium and vitamin D3 is necessary to ensure they receive essential nutrients. Water is obtained from droplets on leaves, which they lick off with their specialized tongue. Misting the enclosure regularly creates these droplets, and a shallow water dish can be provided for drinking.

Handling chameleons should be done with caution, as they are not generally fond of being held and can become stressed when handled excessively. When handling is necessary, it should be gentle, infrequent, and always supporting their body correctly. Minimizing stress is crucial, as stress can lead to health issues.

Monitoring the chameleon's behavior and appearance

is essential for recognizing signs of stress or health problems. Stress indicators may include color changes, aggressive postures, or attempts to escape. In such cases, it's important to minimize handling and assess their living conditions to ensure their comfort. Regular veterinary check-ups and vigilant observation of their behavior, appetite, and appearance can help identify and address health concerns promptly.

Chapter 9

Legal and Ethical Considerations

Laws and Regulations Related to Reptile Ownership

Reptile ownership, like the ownership of any exotic or unconventional pets, is subject to a complex and multifaceted legal landscape. These regulations are implemented at various levels, from local municipalities and states to national authorities, and they encompass a wide array of considerations for responsible ownership.

Local ordinances often serve as the first layer of regulation for reptile ownership. These ordinances can vary significantly from one locality to another. They may dictate if reptiles can be kept as pets and if so, they may specify the types and sizes of reptiles that are allowed within city limits. For example, some cities may have restrictions on large or potentially dangerous reptiles, while others may allow a broader range of species.

State-level regulations are a critical factor in determining what reptiles can be owned legally within a given region. The rules regarding reptile ownership vary widely from state to state. While some states have stringent laws that prohibit the ownership of certain species considered dangerous, others may impose permit requirements, size limitations, or specific enclosures. Understanding these state-level regulations is essential to ensure compliance and responsible ownership.

At the national level, the United States has legislation that can impact reptile ownership. The Lacey Act, for example, prohibits the interstate transportation of wildlife taken in violation of state, tribal, foreign, or other laws. It also addresses the illegal trafficking of endangered species. The Endangered Species Act (ESA) is another federal law that provides protections for reptile species listed as threatened or endangered. Owning, transporting, or trading such species without the appropriate permits is illegal.

Staying informed about changes in legislation is crucial for reptile owners. Laws regarding reptile ownership can evolve over time, so it is essential to remain up to date. Joining or supporting advocacy organizations dedicated to reptile ownership rights can help protect the interests of reptile enthusiasts and ensure that responsible ownership is not compromised. These organizations often play a vital role in monitoring and influencing legislative changes to benefit both reptiles and their owners.

Ethical Sourcing of Reptiles

Ethical sourcing of reptiles is a fundamental aspect of

responsible ownership. It involves acquiring reptiles from reputable breeders and sellers while considering the impact of the pet trade on both individual reptiles and their wild populations.

Identifying reputable breeders and sellers is paramount. Responsible breeders prioritize the health and well-being of their animals and adhere to ethical breeding practices. They provide proper husbandry, nutrition, and veterinary care to their reptiles. Ethical breeders also prioritize the welfare of their breeding stock and ensure that animals are not overbred or subjected to inhumane conditions.

Reputable sellers provide accurate information about the reptiles they offer. They are transparent about the animal's history, health, and any special requirements. Ensuring that the reptiles are legally obtained is a crucial aspect of ethical sourcing. By purchasing from trusted sources, prospective reptile owners contribute to the well-being of the animals and support responsible practices within the pet trade.

Rescue organizations play a vital role in ethical sourcing, especially for species with high demand or those in need of rehoming. These organizations rescue reptiles from various situations, including improper care or abandonment. They provide essential care and rehabilitation, ensuring that rescued reptiles have the opportunity for a better life through adoption. Choosing to adopt from rescue organizations or visiting reptile expositions and shows can be a responsible and compassionate way to acquire a reptile. Responsible pet acquisition also considers the broader impact of the pet trade on specific reptile species and ecosystems. Some reptile species are vulnerable to over-exploitation due to their popularity in the pet trade. Ethical sourcing involves avoiding the acquisition of wild-caught reptiles whenever possible. Captive-bred individuals should be preferred, as they help reduce the pressure on wild populations and promote the responsible ownership of reptiles.

Additionally, responsible reptile owners can support conservation initiatives and efforts aimed at preserving reptile species in the wild. This can include financial contributions to conservation organizations, participation in habitat preservation projects, and even involvement in breeding programs for endangered species.

Conservation Efforts and Responsible Pet Ownership

Responsible pet ownership and conservation efforts are interconnected. The pet trade, if not managed responsibly, can have a significant impact on wild reptile populations, especially for species prone to over-exploitation. Here are some key considerations for reptile owners in supporting conservation:

The pet trade can pose risks to wild populations in several ways. Overcollection of reptiles from their natural habitats can deplete local populations and disrupt ecosystems. Additionally, the demand for specific reptile species can drive illegal trafficking, further threatening these species.

Responsible pet owners play a critical role in conservation efforts. By adhering to ethical sourcing practices and acquiring reptiles through legal and responsible channels, they help reduce the demand for wild-caught reptiles. Supporting captive breeding programs for endangered or threatened species can also contribute to maintaining genetic diversity and reducing pressure on wild populations.

Supporting habitat preservation projects is another way responsible pet owners can contribute to conservation. Many reptile species rely on specific habitats, and the destruction of these habitats can have dire consequences for their survival. By supporting initiatives that protect and restore natural habitats, reptile owners can indirectly help conserve these species.

Responsible reptile owners can also contribute to research efforts aimed at understanding and conserving reptile species facing threats in the wild. Reporting observations of reptile behavior, health, and reproduction can provide valuable data for researchers. Additionally, educational outreach and public awareness efforts can help foster a greater understanding of reptiles and their importance in ecosystems.

Chapter 10

Troubleshooting Guide

Common Problems and Solutions

Reptile ownership can be a rewarding experience, but it also comes with its share of challenges. Understanding and addressing common problems is crucial for ensuring the health and well-being of your reptile companions. In this chapter, the content will explore common issues encountered by reptile owners and offer comprehensive solutions.

One common issue faced by reptile owners is shedding difficulties. Reptiles shed their skin periodically as they grow, but the shedding process can sometimes be problematic. To assist with shedding, provide a humidity-rich environment in your reptile's enclosure. For species with specific shedding preferences, such as soaking in water, ensure access to a suitable shedding aid. Additionally, avoid handling your reptile during the shedding process to prevent damage to their delicate new skin.

Reptiles may occasionally refuse to eat, which can be concerning for owners. The causes of appetite loss can vary by species. It's essential to research your reptile's dietary preferences and nutritional needs. Factors like temperature, lighting, and stress can affect appetite. Ensure that your reptile's enclosure replicates their natural habitat and address any potential stressors. If refusal to eat persists, consult a veterinarian experienced in reptile care for a thorough examination and guidance.

Reptiles exhibit a range of behaviors, and sudden changes can be indicative of underlying issues. Variations in behavior are common among different reptile species, so understanding species-specific behavior is crucial. Behavioral changes, such as increased aggression, unusual activity patterns, or hiding, can signal stress, illness, or environmental factors. Regularly observe your reptile and take note of any deviations from their typical behavior. Address potential stressors, provide appropriate environmental enrichment, and consult a veterinarian if needed.

Reptile owners may encounter other common problems, such as respiratory infections, metabolic issues, or injuries. Ensure that your reptile's enclosure provides optimal temperature, humidity, and lighting conditions. Proper substrate choices, tailored to the preferences of your species, can mitigate substrate-related problems. Vigilance in preventing escape and injury risks through enclosure modifications is essential. Addressing these common issues promptly with the guidance of a reptile veterinarian can help ensure the well-being of your reptile.

Troubleshooting Enclosure Issues

Proper enclosure management is critical for the health and comfort of your reptile. Enclosure issues can lead to stress, illness, and behavioral problems. This section addresses common enclosure-related problems and provides tailored solutions.

Reptiles have specific temperature and humidity requirements, which can vary among species. Ensure that your reptile's enclosure maintains the appropriate temperature gradient, with access to basking spots and cooler areas. Accurate temperature and humidity monitoring tools are essential. For species with specific humidity preferences, such as rainforest-dwellers, use misting systems or humidifiers to maintain suitable humidity levels.

Choosing the right substrate for your reptile is crucial, as inappropriate substrates can lead to issues such as impaction or skin irritation. Research your species' substrate preferences and provide a substrate that aligns with their natural habitat. Remove waste regularly and replace substrates when needed. For species that prefer burrowing, ensure that the substrate depth allows for this behavior safely.

Reptiles can be skilled escape artists, and enclosure modifications may be necessary to prevent escape and injury risks. Tailor your enclosure's design to your species' unique characteristics.

Use secure locks and barriers to prevent escape, especially for more active and agile species. Inspect enclosures regularly for any sharp or hazardous objects that could harm your reptile.

Addressing Behavioral Concerns

Behavioral concerns can arise in reptiles for various reasons, and addressing these issues is essential for their well-being.

Reptiles, especially during breeding seasons, may exhibit aggression or territorial behavior. Mitigating these behaviors involves providing adequate space and environmental enrichment to reduce stress. Separating individuals when necessary and adhering to species-specific recommendations can help manage aggression.

Reptiles may display signs of stress or illness through behavioral changes. These indicators can vary among different species, making it crucial to understand your reptile's specific behavior. Common signs include decreased activity, changes in appetite, lethargy, or unusual postures. If you notice any of these signs, consult a reptile veterinarian promptly to diagnose and address underlying health concerns.

Positive reinforcement techniques can be used to address unusual activity patterns in reptiles. Reward desired behaviors with treats or praise to encourage compliance with handling, training, or other routines. Implementing positive reinforcement requires patience and consistency, as reptiles may have varying responses.

Conclusion

Responsible reptile ownership is a journey filled with unique experiences, challenges, and rewards. As this comprehensive guide to ultimate reptile care concludes, it is important to reflect on the joys and rewards that come with being a responsible reptile owner, reinforcing the commitment to ethical and compassionate care for all covered reptile species.

Each reptile species possesses its own distinctive qualities, behaviors, and characteristics, which make them fascinating and wonderful companions. Whether you've chosen to care for the gentle bearded dragon, the captivating ball python, the charming leopard gecko, or any other reptile species, you've embarked on a journey that allows you to observe and appreciate the marvels of the natural world up close. The bond that forms between a reptile and their owner is a unique and deeply rewarding experience, one that often lasts a lifetime.

In the process of responsible reptile ownership, the guide has delved into the intricacies of creating suitable habitats, understanding dietary needs, addressing health concerns, and fostering positive interactions with reptilian friends. It has explored the legal and ethical considerations surrounding reptile ownership, acknowledging the role in the conservation of these incredible creatures and their habitats.

As responsible reptile owners, we carry the responsibility of providing ethical and compassionate care for our reptile companions. We must continue to prioritize their well-being, seeking knowledge and guidance to ensure that we meet their unique needs. Our commitment extends to supporting conservation initiatives, promoting responsible pet acquisition, and participating in breeding programs when applicable.

In the end, responsible reptile ownership is not just about caring for our reptile friends; it's also about fostering a deep connection with the natural world and becoming advocates for the well-being of these remarkable creatures. It is a journey of discovery, learning, and growth, both for us and for the reptiles we share our lives with.

So, as you embark on this incredible journey of responsible reptile ownership or continue to care for your beloved reptile companions, remember the joys and rewards that come with it. Cherish the moments of observing their unique behaviors and bask in the wonder of their existence. And, above all, let your commitment to ethical and compassionate care be a guiding light on this remarkable path, ensuring that reptiles everywhere receive the love and respect they deserve.

Thank you for choosing to be a responsible reptile owner and for joining us in this celebration of these extraordinary creatures.

www.ingramcontent.com/pod-product-compliance
Lightning Source LLC
LaVergne TN
LVHW020137080526
838202LV00048B/3962